BTEC Apprenticeships

CW01652554

Level 3

MANAGEMENT

Assessment Workbook

BETHAN BITHELL

Welcome to your Assessment Workbook, which will guide and support you as you progress through your apprenticeship. It contains:

- activities to complete that help you to create evidence for assessment
- suggestions for other types of evidence you could collect from your workplace to support your assessment
- information about the practical skills that your assessor may want to see you demonstrate in your workplace
- details of topics that your assessor may want to discuss with you during a visit.

References to criteria appear next to each activity so you and your assessor can see at a glance what is covered.

Good luck!

www.btecapprenticeships.com

ALWAYS LEARNING

PEARSON

Published by Pearson Education Limited, a company incorporated in England and Wales, having its registered office at Edinburgh Gate, Harlow, Essex, CM20 2JE. Registered company number: 872828

www.pearsonschoolsandfecolleges.co.uk
Text © Pearson Education Limited 2012
Content of pages 115–150 © Business Skills @ Work, 2010
Designed by Pearson Education Ltd
Typeset by Tek-Art, Crawley Down, West Sussex
Original illustrations © Pearson Education Ltd
Cover photo/illustration © Corbis: Westend61

The right of Bethan Bithell to be identified as author of this work has been asserted by her in accordance with the Copyright, Designs and Patents Act 1988

First published 2012

15 14 13
10 9 8 7 6 5 4 3 2

British Library Cataloguing in Publication Data
A catalogue record for this book is available from the British Library

ISBN 978 1 446902 68 4

Printed and bound in the UK by Ashford Colour Press

Acknowledgements
The publisher would like to thank the following individuals and organisations for permission to reproduce photographs:

(Key: b-bottom; c-centre; l-left; r-right; t-top)

Alamy Images: Goodshot / Jupiter Images 69t, Stockbroker / MBI 56t, Tetra Images 114t; **Corbis:** Colorblind 38t, Corbis: 33t, ERproductions Ltd / Blend Images 82c, Helen King 94b, 112t, JLP / Jose L. Pelaez 72b, Monty Rakusen / cultura 50t, Tim Pannell 93t; **Getty Images:** altrendo images 70b, Bambu Productions 64b, Jose Luis Pelaez 47t, Mark Williamson 14b, Michael Rosenfeld 1, Sean Ellis 12tl, Smith Collection 18c; **Pearson Education Ltd:** Lord and Leverett 25b; **Shutterstock.com:** auremar 109t, Brian A Jackson 90b, Kotofot 3b, Stocklite 115t; **SuperStock:** Corbis 27t, Image Source 100t, Stockbroker 105b

All other images © Pearson Education

Picture research: Sally Cole

Every effort has been made to trace the copyright holders and we apologise in advance for any unintentional omissions. We would be pleased to insert the appropriate acknowledgement in any subsequent edition of this publication.

Websites
Pearson Education Limited is not responsible for the content of any external internet sites. It is essential for tutors to preview each website before using it in class so as to ensure that the URL is still accurate, relevant and appropriate. We suggest that tutors bookmark useful websites and consider enabling students to access them through the institution's intranet.

Disclaimer
This material has been published on behalf of Edexcel and offers high-quality support for the delivery of Edexcel qualifications.

This does not mean that the material is essential to achieve any Edexcel qualification, nor does it mean that it is the only suitable material available to support any Edexcel qualification. Material from this publication will not be used verbatim in any examination or assessment set by Edexcel. Any resource lists produced by Edexcel shall include this and other appropriate resources.

Copies of official specifications for all Edexcel qualifications may be found on the Edexcel website: www.edexcel.com

Additional support for using this Assessment Workbook is available from www.btecapprenticeshipworkbooks.co.uk

Username: manage3
Password: man3learn

BTEC APPRENTICESHIP LEVEL 3 MANAGEMENT

Apprentice name	
Apprentice number	
Assessor name	
Training provider	
Employer	

The candidate has successfully completed all relevant sections of the BTEC Apprenticeship Assessment Workbook	
Assessor's signature:	**Date:**
I confirm that all the work submitted is my own and that all sources of information have been fully acknowledged	
Apprentice's signature:	**Date:**

INTRODUCTION TO YOUR BTEC APPRENTICESHIP

There is a glossary on page x explaining key terms that you will come across frequently during your Apprenticeship. These words appear in **bold** when they first come up in this introduction.

An Apprenticeship is a work-based qualification. While you are working for your employer and developing your skills and knowledge in the workplace, you will also have regular contact with an **assessor**. Your assessor will support you in your learning and assessment, possibly sometimes at a local college or training centre.

Your Level 3 BTEC Apprenticeship in Management may consist of the following qualifications:

- NVQ Level 3 Certificate in Management
- BTEC Level 3 Certificate in Management
- BTEC WorkSkills for Effective Learning and Employment
- Functional Skills at Level 2 in English, mathematics and ICT
- **OR** Essential Skills Wales in Communication, Application of Number and ICT at Level 2 (if you are based in Wales)
- Employment Responsibilities and Rights
- Personal, Learning and Thinking Skills (in England only)

All of these qualifications, apart from Functional Skills, can be assessed through practical work-based activities, evidence of what you do in your day-to-day job, and discussions and observations with your assessor.

ASSESSMENT

This Assessment Workbook will help you make the most of the different assessment options that are available for your Apprenticeship. You may be assessed through:

- work tasks that let you demonstrate your **competence**
- **observations** of you completing work tasks
- discussions with your assessor that demonstrate your knowledge and understanding
- written **evidence**, for example completed Knowledge and Understanding pages from this Assessment Workbook.

Any assessment work will need to be recorded for your **portfolio**. Your assessor will advise you of the best methods of recording this evidence. Because you may work with confidential information, your portfolio should contain the location of any naturally occurring workplace evidence (such as letters or reports) rather than a copy of the documents themselves.

Your assessor will let you know if any of the units in the BTEC Certificate will be assessed using onscreen tests. If you are being assessed onscreen, you may find the interactive quizzes provided at www.btecapprenticeshipworkbooks.co.uk help prepare you for the test.

Your assessor will help you select the units of the different qualifications that best suit your needs and the needs of your employer. This Assessment Workbook does not cover every optional unit in the qualification, so your assessor will let you know which sections of the Workbook are most relevant for your Apprenticeship.

As part of your Apprenticeship, you will need to pass the Functional Skills qualifications listed above. These are assessed through timed tests, which may be paper-based or onscreen. Your assessor will advise you of when you will sit these and will help you prepare for the assessment. You can find practice assessment papers at www.btecapprenticeshipworkbooks.co.uk. If you are taking Essential Skills Wales instead, your assessor will discuss with you when and how you will complete this assessment.

THE ROLE OF YOUR EMPLOYER

During your BTEC Apprenticeship, your employer needs to provide you with:

- enough time to allow you to complete your Apprenticeship work
- opportunities to demonstrate the necessary skills in your workplace
- a mentor to help provide informal training and support
- a wage.

In addition, your employer (or your colleagues) may support you in completing your Apprenticeship through:

- providing **witness statements** that can be used as evidence for your Apprenticeship
- additional training where you need to develop your skills and knowledge further
- support and guidance if you have any human resources issues.

THE ROLE OF YOUR ASSESSOR

Your assessor will support you in completing your BTEC Apprenticeship. He or she will visit you at your workplace and discuss the Apprenticeship with you to make sure qualifications are suitable for your needs and job role, and that you fully understand what you will need to learn and do during the Apprenticeship programme.

During your Apprenticeship, your assessor needs to:

- make sure you understand how you will be assessed and what you will be assessed on
- give you good notice of each time they visit you at your workplace, and what you need to have completed in preparation for the visit
- discuss your work and your job role with your employer and colleagues to gather additional evidence for your portfolio.

In addition, your assessor may recommend supporting resources, such as textbooks or e-learning, that you need to use during the course of the Apprenticeship to help you build your knowledge and skills.

YOUR ROLE

You are responsible for both carrying out the job that your employer is paying you to do and for completing your Apprenticeship. Your responsibilities to your employer are:

- to do the work required of you to a satisfactory standard
- to keep your employer informed of how you are progressing through the Apprenticeship
- to meet the general requirements of an employee at your workplace (for example, to turn up on time).

You also have responsibilities to your assessor. Your assessor will need you to:

- inform your employer of the dates when your assessor is visiting you at your workplace
- complete the work required of you by the date agreed, and if you are unable to do so, keep your assessor informed of your progress
- attend any training organised by your **training provider**
- keep them informed of the work activities you are planning to carry out on the dates of your assessor visits – if you will not be in the workplace on that day, tell your assessor as soon as possible so they can reschedule the visit
- make sure your work is your own and that you indicate the original source of any information or wording that you have found somewhere else (for example, on the Internet).

HOW TO USE THIS BTEC APPRENTICESHIP ASSESSMENT WORKBOOK

This BTEC Apprenticeship Assessment Workbook has been designed to support you and your assessor in completing your BTEC Apprenticeship. It helps you to prove your knowledge, understanding and skills, and identify evidence that will demonstrate your competence and go towards achieving your Apprenticeship.

As you will be submitting this Assessment Workbook to your assessor as evidence for your Apprenticeship, you need to make sure you keep it safe and update it regularly.

WHAT THE ASSESSMENT WORKBOOK COVERS

Your assessor will discuss your Apprenticeship with you and will identify a number of units that will be relevant to you and your job role. This Assessment Workbook covers all the mandatory units and a selection of optional to complete the qualifications that make up the BTEC Apprenticeship.

	Credits	Mandatory/ Optional
BTEC Level 3 Certificate in Management		
Unit 1: Key principles of management and leadership	5	M
Unit 2: Improving your own management and leadership performance	2	M
Unit 3: Managing the delivery of customer service	3	O
Unit 5: Appraising and developing staff	3	O
Unit 9: Developing working relationships with team members	3	O
NVQ Level 3 Certificate in Management		
Unit 1: Manage own professional development within an organisation	4	M
Unit 2: Set objectives and provide support for team members	5	M
Unit 3: Plan, allocate and monitor work of a team	5	M
Unit 5: Provide leadership and direction for own area of responsibility	5	O
Unit 15: Develop working relationships with colleagues	3	O
Unit 18: Address performance problems affecting team members	3	O
Unit 40: Manage customer service in own area of responsibility	4	O
Level 3 Workskills for Effective Learning and Employment		
Unit 1: Preparing for a Level 3 Apprenticeship	1	M
Unit 5: Using research skills to solve problems (CT/IE)	1	O
Unit 6: Participating through team leading (EP/TW)	1	O
Unit 7: Manage own learning (RL/SM)	1	O
Unit 9: Understanding employment responsibilities and rights	3	O

The Assessment Workbook also covers the Employment Rights and Responsibilities (ERR) and Personal, Learning and Thinking Skills (PLTS) requirements set by the Standard Setting Body for an Apprenticeship in Management. The last section of the Workbook is the same as the ERR Workbook available from the Council for Administration (CfA), so if you complete this the CfA will accept it as evidence of your knowledge of ERR.

Your assessor also has separate information showing how you can prove your basic skills if you are taking Essential Skills Wales qualifications.

USING THE BTEC APPRENTICESHIP ASSESSMENT WORKBOOK

The Assessment Workbook contains a mixture of activities and guidance, which combine **assessment criteria** from these different qualifications and involve real work activities related to your day-to-day job. Your assessor will suggest which activities and sections you should complete and read at each point of your Apprenticeship. Use the activities and guidance to create or collect evidence, and to prepare for observations and **professional discussions** when your assessor visits you in your workplace.

In the margins of the Assessment Workbook you will see references to the assessment criteria covered (or partially covered) by each activity. The following abbreviations have been used:

- BTEC = BTEC Level 3 Certificate
- NVQ = NVQ Level 3 Certificate
- WorkSkills = WorkSkills for Effective Learning and Employment
- PLTS = Personal, Learning and Thinking Skills

The different activities and information in the Assessment Workbook are as follows.

KNOWLEDGE AND UNDERSTANDING TASKS

Complete these tasks to produce evidence of your knowledge and understanding of the different parts of your Apprenticeship. This may involve talking to your colleagues or manager, and will normally be completed before your assessor visits you in your workplace. Before each assessor visit, your assessor will discuss with you which activities they want you to complete.

You will also find electronic versions of these tasks online at www.btecapprenticeshipworkbooks.co.uk ready for you to type into and save. Your assessor will discuss with you how to complete the tasks this way.

EVIDENCE GATHERING

Use this information to identify where what you do in your everyday work can form part of the evidence you can submit for your Apprenticeship. This evidence needs to fit certain requirements, which are listed here, so make sure you check your evidence against these before including it in your portfolio.

PUTTING IT INTO PRACTICE

These sections prepare you for **observations**, when your assessor may want to observe you at work during their visits. Your assessor may also ask you questions about what you're doing to check your understanding, so make sure you read through the preparation notes provided here. They will discuss with you which of these sections you should read, depending on which work activities you are going to be carrying out when they next visit you at your workplace.

PROFESSIONAL DISCUSSION

Your assessor will carry out, and record, professional discussions with you to check your knowledge, understanding and skills. They may combine the professional discussions from more than one section of the Assessment Workbook if they want to discuss several topics at the same time. These sections will help you prepare for discussion when your assessor visits you at your workplace.

www.btecapprenticeshipworkbooks.co.uk

There is a website that accompanies this Assessment Workbook, which contains the following additional support for you:

- Interactive revision activities to help you prepare for onscreen assessment for certain units. (Your assessor will discuss and agree with you if you are going to use this kind of assessment.) You can, of course, also use these revision quizzes to check your knowledge if you are not using onscreen assessment.
- Electronic copies of the Knowledge and Understanding tasks from the Assessment Workbook that you can complete and save. You may need the latest version of Adobe Acrobat Reader to use these. The free software can be downloaded from http://get.adobe.com/reader/
- Practice Functional Skills activities to help you develop your skills and prepare you for the test.

To log on to this website:

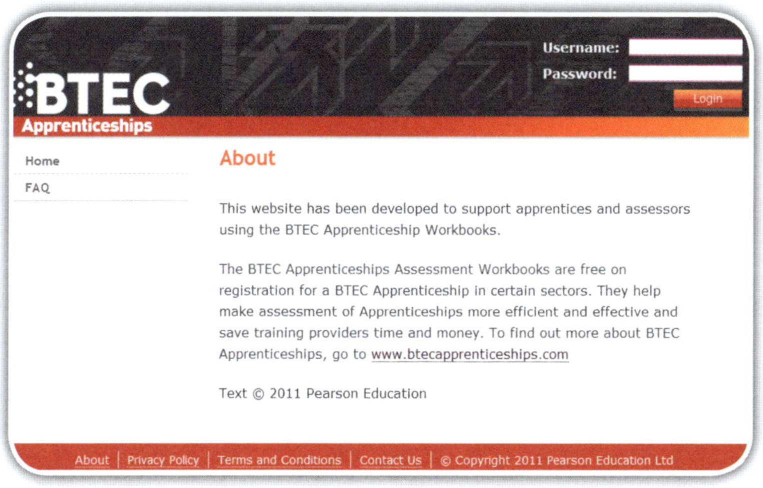

1. Go to www.btecapprenticeshipworkbooks.co.uk
2. In the login box on the top-right corner of your screen, use the following login details:
   Username: manage3
   Password: man3learn
3. Click on "Login". You will then be able to select the support materials you want to use.

GLOSSARY

Below is a list of key terms that you will come across frequently in your Apprenticeship and the BTEC Apprenticeship Assessment Workbook.

Assessment criteria – statements within a unit of a qualification describing the standards by which your skills or knowledge will be measured.

Assessor – the person from your training provider who will visit you in your workplace; their role is to support you through your Apprenticeship and to assess your performance and knowledge.

Competence – your skills and abilities in performing your work; competence means having the necessary knowledge and skills for your role.

Evidence – anything that demonstrates you have the knowledge, understanding and skills specified in the assessment criteria.

Learning outcome – statements within a unit of a qualification describing what you will have learned or be able to do once you have completed part of a unit.

Observation – your assessor will watch you carrying out practical activities and parts of your job in order to judge your competence and will then keep a formal record of your performance.

Portfolio – you and your assessor will need to record and organise the items of evidence you gather during your apprenticeship; a portfolio helps you to keep everything together and allows you to monitor your progress over time. Some training providers use paper-based portfolios, while others use e-portfolios, in which your evidence is recorded and stored digitally.

Professional discussion – a structured conversation with your assessor that allows you to demonstrate your understanding of work practice or procedures and may also enable you to provide evidence of knowledge or competence.

Training provider – a college or private training organisation responsible for assessing your competence in your workplace and, where necessary, for delivering additional training to develop your knowledge and skills.

Witness statement – a statement that can support your evidence of competence, from a person who is qualified to make comments about your performance (for example, your manager). It must include: a description of the activity you have carried out; how it relates to the assessment criteria; when and in what context the activity was carried out.

1

Your initial induction session is likely to be scheduled to take place at the very beginning of your Apprenticeship period, but an induction is really an ongoing process that allows you to update and develop yourself continually as you work through your Apprenticeship.

Your Apprenticeship induction is a process designed to give you the opportunity to show your knowledge and understanding of the following:

1. You and your employment
2. You and your assessment process

At your initial induction session, your assessor and line manager will ensure that you understand what is expected of you during your time as an apprentice.

In this section you will find a range of activities to help you prepare and gather evidence for your assessment in relation to the following topics:

- the terms and conditions of your contract of employment
- your rights and responsibilities
- the rights and responsibilities of your employer

- areas of equality and diversity
- your organisation's policies and procedures
- the importance of data protection
- health and safety concerns
- you and your organisation.

Your induction process may explore the following:

- agreeing methods for contacting your assessor and internal verifiers
- the process of internal and external verification
- your responsibilities as a candidate
- your training provider's responsibilities
- an assessment appeals procedure
- how to avoid plagiarism
- the availability of learner support
- evidence gathering (including the meaning of the terms 'sufficient', 'relevant', 'current' and 'authentic')
- how to approach the sets of activities in your workbook
- the benefits of electronic and/or paper-based methods of assessment.

In addition, your assessor may wish to conduct a 'skill scan' with you, to establish and agree the choice of optional units that you will work on.

1. YOU AND YOUR EMPLOYMENT

1

Your initial induction session will take place during Visit 1. You will be given the opportunity to talk to your assessor and line manager and to ask any questions you may have in relation to your job role and future development opportunities. You can also discuss the support you can expect to receive from your appointed workplace mentor.

TERMS AND CONDITIONS OF EMPLOYMENT

There are certain things that both you and your employer are automatically entitled to or can reasonably expect. These are known as 'rights'. Similarly, both you and your employer have obligations placed upon you, and these are known as 'responsibilities'.

Your employer is obliged by law to give you written details of your contract of employment within eight weeks of commencing work. However, from a legal point of view, you will already be in a contract

By signing a contract, both you and your employer are agreeing to the terms and conditions of your employment.

1

with your new employer, as you will have been offered a position which you have chosen to accept and you have turned up for work on your first day.

The document (contract of employment) that you will receive within eight weeks should clearly inform you of your terms and conditions of employment, and during your initial induction session your employer may wish to discuss these in more depth, giving you the opportunity to ask questions to clarify any points you are unsure of.

Your terms and conditions of employment may include, for example, procedures for reporting sickness, holiday entitlement, and which day of the month you will get paid.

KNOWLEDGE AND UNDERSTANDING

WorkSkills Unit 9: 2.1

Task 1a

Use the space in the table below to record as many terms and conditions of employment as you can and explain what each means for you. (An example is given to start you off.)

My terms and conditions of employment		
Item	**Description**	**What it means for me / what actions I should take**
Example: **1.** *Sickness leave*	*The procedures to follow if you are ill on days when you should be at work*	*I must inform the organisation by 10.00am on my first day of sickness that I am unable to attend work*
2.		
3.		
4.		
5.		

Item	Description	What it means for me / what actions I should take
6.		
7.		
8.		
9.		
10.		

WorkSkills Unit 9: 2.3

Task 1b

Now, take steps to find information that will help you to answer the following:

What are the procedures you would need to follow in the event of a grievance?

1

WorkSkills Unit 9: 2.5

Task 1c

Next, take steps to find information that will help you to answer the following:

If you are unable to work due to sickness, what are the arrangements you must make with your doctor to satisfy your employer?

WorkSkills Unit 9: 1.1, 1.2

Task 1d

Now, carry out some research that will help you to answer the following:

Explain briefly the impact of the Working Time Directive on your working hours.

Rights and responsibilities

Both you and your employer have rights (things you are automatically entitled to) and also responsibilities (obligations placed upon you).

Without rights and responsibilities there would be little structure to your working day and there would always be the possibility that one party in the contract could take advantage of the other party.

For example, it is the responsibility of your employer to ensure you work in a safe and healthy environment, while it is your responsibility to make sure you turn up for work on time every day.

Similarly, your employer has the right to dismiss an employee (using correct procedures) if there is a case of serious misconduct, while you have the right to be paid on time.

Employment law

Employment law is changing all the time. To be able to keep up to date with changes to the legislation you can access the following online organisations:

- Business Link http://www.businesslink.gov.uk/bdotg/action/home
- Direct Gov http://www.direct.gov.uk/en/index.htm
- ACAS http://www.acas.org.uk/index.aspx?articleid=1461

Employment law covers all aspects of your employment, from how much you should get paid to how you should be treated. Aspects of employment law include:

- equal opportunities
- grievance and disciplinary issues
- contract of employment
- unfair dismissal
- maternity and paternity pay
- hours of work.

WorkSkills Unit 9: 1.1, 1.3

Task 2a

Spend some time thinking about rights and responsibilities. You may ask other people around you for ideas and then formulate your own thoughts to complete the table below. List the rights and responsibilities that employers have, and then list the employee's rights and responsibilities.

My employer's rights and responsibilities

1

My rights and responsibilities

WorkSkills Unit 9: 1.4

Task 2b

Carry out some research into organisations that may represent employees or provide support in relation to workplace situations. List your findings below. (Two examples are given to start you off.)

Name of representative body	Support given
1. *The Health and Safety Executive (HSE)*	*Will investigate unsafe practices and accidents*
2. *Citizens Advice Bureau (CAB)*	*Can offer advice on employment issues*
3.	
4.	
5.	
6.	

Areas of equality and diversity

Now carry out some research into the protection that employees are given. Find out the names of the laws in relation to equal opportunities. Laws made by the Government such as the Equality Act 2010 are often referred to as statutes or Acts of Parliament.

Equality Act 2010

The Equality Act 2010 has replaced previous anti-discrimination laws in order to make the law easier to understand and comply with. This Act covers nine protected characteristics:

1. age
2. disability
3. gender reassignment
4. marriage and civil partnership
5. pregnancy and maternity
6. race
7. religion and belief
8. sex
9. sexual orientation.

The key purpose of this Act is to prevent anybody from treating another person unfairly. This includes direct and indirect discrimination, victimisation, harassment and not making reasonable adjustments for a disabled person (such as access to a building).

WorkSkills Unit 9: 1.1

Task 3a

Now answer the two questions below.

1. What is meant by 'indirect discrimination'?

1

2. What is meant by 'direct discrimination'?

WorkSkills Unit 9: 1.2

Task 3b

Find your workplace Equality and Diversity policy and any procedures that relate to equal opportunities, and read them carefully. Once you have done this, answer the following questions:

1. How do you ensure that you are up to date with amendments to equality, diversity and inclusion policies and procedures as set by your organisation?

2. When planning team meetings or allocating work to your team, how do you ensure your organisation's equality, diversity and inclusion procedures are implemented, and how would you monitor this?

WorkSkills Unit 9: 1.2

Task 3c

What does your organisation do to ensure it works within the boundaries of the Equality Act 2010? Using the table below, explain how your organisation is complying with the listed characteristics.

Characteristic	How your organisation is complying with the legislation
Disability	
Race	
Religion and belief	
Age	
Pregnancy and maternity	

WorkSkills Unit 9: 1.2, 2.5

Task 3d

List six policies and/or organisational processes within your organisation that ensure equality, diversity and inclusion. Provide a brief description of the purpose of these. If your organisation has fewer than six, suggest others that you could include.

Area needing protection, for example disability	Policy and/or procedure	Description
	1.	
	2.	
	3.	
	4.	
	5.	
	6.	

1

A workplace policy will outline the rules about the place where you work, and may dictate what you are and are not allowed to do and where.

WorkSkills Unit 9: 2.5

Your organisation's policies and procedures

A workplace policy is a document written by senior managers stating what can or cannot be done in a particular workplace. An example would be a smoking policy. This would state clearly where (and when) smoking can take place and where it cannot take place. This process ensures that employees know what is expected of them in terms of their behaviour while they are working.

Procedures are often referred to as a list of step by step instructions that everyone should follow. This means that everyone in the organisation – including temporary workers – operates in exactly the same way when carrying out tasks such as completing paperwork, answering the telephone or using equipment. This process reduces the possibility of mistakes being made and also reduces the amount of waste in the organisation.

Task 4

Identify the policies and procedures that exist in your workplace and then complete the table below.

Name of workplace *policy*	What it informs employees of
1.	
2.	
3.	
4.	
5.	

Name of workplace *procedure*	What it informs employees of
1.	
2.	
3.	
4.	
5.	

The importance of data protection in your workplace

The Government introduced the Data Protection Act in 1984 to ensure that information held about individuals on workplace computerised systems would not reach other people or organisations, without the individual's permission. The Act was updated in 1998, and it allows individuals to request to see the information held about them by organisations.

The Data Protection Act governs the use of personal information through eight data protection principles, which state that personal information should be:

1. processed fairly and lawfully
2. processed for a limited purpose
3. adequate, relevant and not excessive
4. accurate and up to date
5. not kept for longer than is necessary
6. processed in line with the rights of individuals
7. secure
8. not transferred to other countries without adequate protection.

The Data Protection Act protects personal information. This is data about living, identified or identifiable individuals.

WorkSkills Unit 9: 2.4

Task 5a

Give three examples of personal information that must be kept up to date with your employer.

1.

2.

3.

1

WorkSkills Unit 9: 2.4

Task 5b

The personal information that your employer holds about you must be kept up-to-date and accurate. In the space below, identify the personal information your employer will have on record.

Discuss your answers with your assessor or line manager.

Health and safety in your workplace

The Health and Safety at Work Act 1974 is what the Government refers to as an 'enabling' act. This means that since 1974, the Government has been able to strengthen the areas that the Act covers by introducing a series of additional regulations to try to make sure everyone is as safe and healthy as possible at work.

There will be many regulations and codes of practice in your workplace introduced or designed to offer protection to all. It is worth noting, however, that the Health and Safety at Work Act 1974 (known as HASAW) indicates that it is the responsibility of both the employer and employee to ensure the safety of themselves and everyone else around them in the workplace.

Employers should position signage in the workplace so that employees/visitors know what must be done to keep everyone safe.

You will need to know the health and safety regulations and codes of practice that affect you in your own workplace.

WorkSkills Unit 9: 1.1, 1.2, 1.3

Task 6

Answer the following questions:

Give two examples of health and safety regulations that apply to your own work role (for example, Noise at Work Regulations).

1.

2.

If there is a fire at your workplace and you have to leave the building because of it, where should you congregate with your colleagues outside?

You and your organisation

Your contract of employment is a legal agreement between you and your employer. Basically, you provide your skills and services to your employer who, in exchange, pays you a sum of money each month for those skills and services.

Your wages are likely to be paid directly into your bank account, but the law states that your employer should make sure that you receive a payslip each month which shows how much you have earned, how much has been deducted by your employer and what those deductions are.

WorkSkills Unit 9: 2.2

Task 7

List three items that you would find on your payslip and briefly describe their meaning (for example, your National Insurance Number).

1.

2.

3.

1

Understanding how your own job role fits within your organisation is vital to achieve organisational targets. Your job description outlines your tasks and responsibilities and, in addition, your regular meetings with your manager will set out how your team objectives will contribute to the organisation's objectives.

WorkSkills Unit 9: 3.1

Task 8a

Now think about your own role in your workplace.

Examine the job description you have been given and list your main tasks/activities.

WorkSkills Unit 9: 3.1, 3.2, 3.3, 3.4, 3.5

Task 8b

In view of your response above, answer the following questions.

1. How does your own role contribute to the overall targets that your organisation has to meet?

2. How does your own role compare with similar roles of those working in other organisations in the sector?

3. How would you describe the way members of the public think about the work that your organisation does? (For instance, do they think the work is dangerous or causes pollution?)

4. Reflect on your responses to question 3 above, and describe how issues of public concern have altered public views of the sector you work within.

5. Describe what the roles and responsibilities are likely to be of a representative body that supports the industry sector you work in.

6. How does the representative body you have chosen in question 5 support the industry sector you work in?

1

2. YOU AND YOUR ASSESSMENT PROCESS

Your assessor will discuss your assessment process in detail with you and your workplace mentor or line manager.

The purpose of this part of your induction is to make sure you understand how you will be assessed, where assessment will take place and how often. You will also be informed of the support that is available to you during your Apprenticeship period.

Note: It is likely that your assessor will refer to your Apprenticeship Agreement at this stage.

Your assessor will talk you through the assessment process during your induction period.

At the end of this part of your induction process your assessor will have discussed with you:

- the importance of meeting your agreed assessment deadlines
- the importance of being well organised to help you to meet your assessment deadlines
- how each component of your Apprenticeship framework will be assessed
- your 'next steps' for progression, upon successful completion of this Apprenticeship framework.

The pages that follow will enable you and your assessor to discuss the above points in more detail.

HOW YOUR ASSESSMENT PROCESS WILL WORK

Initially, your assessor will agree and then confirm with you the units you will be expected to undertake.

Your assessor will then explain whether your assessment process will be by a paper-based or electronic method or perhaps a combination of both. The sets of activities contained in your Workbook will also be fully explained.

WorkSkills Unit 1: 1.2

Task 1a

As a result of your discussion with your assessor about the process of evidence gathering, write a brief explanation of each of the following terms:

Sufficient

Relevant

Current

Authentic

WorkSkills Unit 1: 1.2

Task 1b

Now write a brief explanation of why your assessor felt it was important to discuss confidentiality for when you gather evidence.

1

WorkSkills Unit 1: 1.1, 1.2

Task 1c

Having discussed your assessment process and needs with your assessor and workplace mentor or line manager, and having researched further if necessary, now take some time to answer the following questions in relation to assessment:

The components of my Apprenticeship are:

1.

2.

3.

4.

5.

Three of my responsibilities as an Apprenticeship framework candidate are:

1.

2.

3.

Three of the responsibilities of my training provider are:

1.

2.

3.

The sets of activities I will undertake in my workbook will include:

1.

2.

3.

4.

Plagiarism means:

An internal verifier is a person who:

An external verifier is a person who:

A skill scan is a process of:

My training provider will provide candidate learner support if I need it. This support may include:

If I think I need learner support, I should speak to:

Name:

Role:

1

My assessor has explained to me that an assessment appeal procedure would work as follows:

WorkSkills Unit 1: 2.2, 2.3

Task 1d

The table below is set out using headings that will enable you to develop SMART targets to assist you in completing your Apprenticeship. The acronym SMART stands for:

- Specific
- Measurable
- Achievable
- Realistic
- Time-bound.

Using the table below, identify what you will need to do to complete your Apprenticeship and when your actions need to be done by. (An example has been done for you.)

Task	Learning and development need	Resources needed (including time)	By when	Review date
Attend 'How to conduct appraisals' internal training	*How to conduct personal development review meetings effectively*	*Time to attend training, PDR documentation*	*31 March 2013*	*1 April 2013*

WorkSkills Unit 1: 2.1

Task 1e

In the space below, state why it is important for you to manage your time effectively to ensure you complete your apprenticeship on time.

Information about progression routes

Once you have completed your Level 3 Apprenticeship, there are many options available to you. Finding the most suitable route will depend on your needs and the guidance and support you receive from various people and organisations.

You can obtain information about progression routes from:

- your Human Resources department
- your manager
- your mentor
- your careers advisers
- your college
- your local university
- your awarding body
- Citizens Advice Bureau
- internet career advice sites
- Directgov website
- friends and family
- your local job centre.

WorkSkills Unit 1: 3.1, 3.2

Task 1f

What route of progression would you like to pursue once you have completed this Apprenticeship? Identify two possible routes.

1.

2.

Where will you obtain relevant information about your chosen progression routes?

1

Assess how useful the information you have obtained is to enable you to consider your progression routes.

Using the progression routes you have identified above, analyse the appropriateness of these routes. Are they realistic? Please provide reasons for your answers.

Route 1:

Route 2:

If for any reason my assessor or I are unable to keep to agreed appointments, the procedure and processes to follow are:

a. If I can't keep an agreed appointment or arranged visit, I will:

b. If my assessor can't keep an agreed appointment or arranged visit, they will:

1

PROFESSIONAL DISCUSSION

WorkSkills Unit 1: 1.1, 1.2, 1.3

Your responsibilities as an Apprenticeship framework candidate

Your assessor will discuss with you what they expect from you as a candidate. These expectations are likely to include that:

- you know the components of your Apprenticeship
- you are committed to making sure all activities are approached with enthusiasm and to best of your ability
- you meet all agreed assessment deadlines (and understand the importance of doing so)
- the work you produce is your own and is not copied from or taken from any other source (this is called plagiarism)
- researched work is referenced properly
- you make sure you are available for agreed visits and appointments
- you regularly attend agreed training sessions arranged on-site or at your training provider's premises.

You can expect your assessor to take steps to ensure that you fully understand each of the above.

Listening to feedback from your assessor will help you get the most out of your apprenticeship journey.

Your training provider's responsibilities

Your assessor will also explain to you what you can reasonably expect from your training provider. Your expectations may include:

- a suitably qualified, approachable and competent assessor
- a training provider that promotes fairness and equality for all of its candidates
- a training provider that has fully equipped educational premises that operate in accordance with appropriate health and safety laws
- a training provider that meets fully the expectations of the awarding bodies it works with and meets quality standards as assessed by the Government and other bodies
- suitable and appropriate learning materials to be supplied to you on a timely basis
- feedback from your assessor on a timely basis for your learning activities
- full support for you as appropriate (for example, in using IT, writing assignments, spelling) from your training provider's staff.

We, the undersigned, agree that a comprehensive induction programme has been undertaken in relation to employment and assessment processes.		
1. The Apprentice		
Name:	Signature:	Date:
2. The workplace mentor / line manager		
Name:	Signature:	Date:
3. The assessor		
Name:	Signature:	Date:
4. The internal verifier		
Name:	Signature:	Date:

2

With your initial induction session complete, you can now prepare for your next assessor visit. The pages that follow will serve as a guide to help you.

In this section you will find a range of activities to help you prepare and gather evidence for your assessment, in relation to:

1. Assessing and developing your management skills

Evaluating the skills and knowledge required for effective leadership and management will enable you to develop a plan to help you focus on your personal career goals. It is important to understand that the success of your team and its ability to meet targets and satisfy customers' needs largely depends upon your ability to perform well as a manager.

The activities that follow will enable you to identify and discuss the requirements of your work role with your line manager and assessor.

Your assessor may need to visit you at your workplace to observe you carrying out real-life activities that may provide evidence for assessment purposes. Please be aware that you should check with colleagues that they have no objection to observations or recordings taking place while they are present. Also, it is always a good idea to inform your manager of the date and time that your assessor is due to visit.

It may also be necessary for your assessor to meet with your line manager to obtain a witness statement to confirm some aspects of the framework. This is nothing to worry about, but it would be a good idea to let your manager know the date of the planned visit well in advance.

1. ASSESSING AND DEVELOPING YOUR MANAGEMENT SKILLS

KNOWLEDGE AND UNDERSTANDING

1. Performance management

Depending upon the structure of an organisation, there may be employees who work as managers and other employees who work as team leaders. This can seem confusing, as it appears to suggest that management and leadership are two separate roles within an organisation. Many management theorists, however, say that management and leadership are really the same thing and that 'leadership' should be considered one part of the 'management' process.

Knowledge and skills required for effective management and leadership

Often leadership is described as directing and instructing people and making vital decisions on behalf of the organisation. This is true – but an effective leader also possesses a number of other skills.

To be an effective leader it is necessary to have respect and trust from your staff, whereas management is also about the ability to deal with organisational processes, policies and procedures. Consider the comparison below:

- Management is being able to manage organisational processes, being an effective planner, using organisational systems and being an effective communicator.

- Leadership is being able to earn trust and respect from your team, and being able to inspire your team to get the job done.

Examples of leadership qualities are:

- integrity
- honesty
- confidence
- courage
- commitment
- passion
- sensitivity
- determination.

Examples of management skills are:

- time management
- planning skills
- financial management
- communication skills
- organisational skills
- writing skills.

Your leadership and management behaviours can be developed over time and it is important that your team members find you approachable at all times – even when you may be feeling stressed or under pressure yourself! Some of the leadership and management tasks you will need to consider are listed below:

- coaching and mentoring others
- planning work and setting objectives
- supporting others
- communicating effectively
- leading by example
- managing disagreement and conflict
- influencing and persuading others
- motivating your team members
- measuring performance and obtaining feedback
- solving problems
- delegation
- promoting a culture of quality
- promoting fairness and equality.

Leadership is often described as influencing and inspiring others and creating a vision for them, while management is often described as the planning, coordinating and controlling of activities. You may find it helpful to think of behaviours rather than tasks. Leadership behaviours should form part of the management process.

2

BTEC Unit 1: 1.2

Task 1a

Think carefully about your management and leadership skills and complete the table below. Think about which skills you currently possess and those skills you wish to develop further. Describe what each of the skills here involve.

Leadership and Management skills	A skill I possess or wish to develop	Description
Ability to influence others		
Ability to inspire others		
Ability to encourage others to develop their skills		
Ability to plan work effectively		
Ability to organise and coordinate activities		
Ability to motivate others by creating a vision		

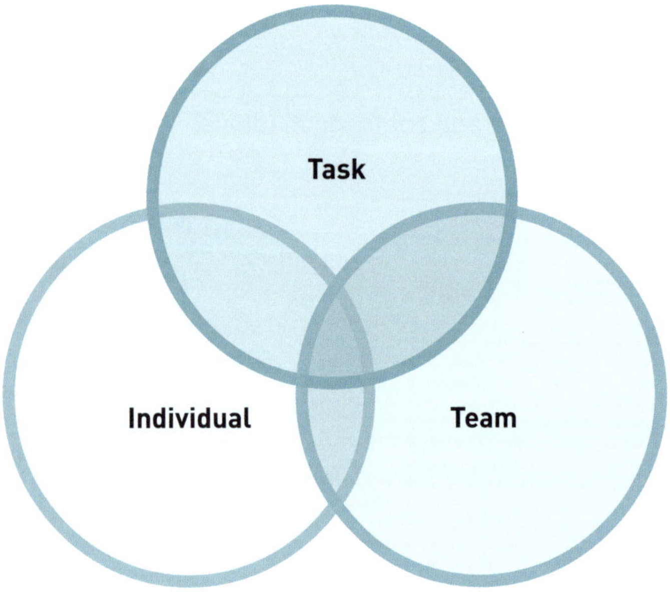

John Adair's Action-centred leadership model identifies three core management responsibilities, and shows how these overlap.

You may discuss with your assessor or line manager the skills you identified from the list above that you wish to develop further.

John Adair's Action-centred leadership model

It's often useful to examine the work of management theorists to recognise the importance of management and leadership skills. John Adair's Action-centred leadership model offers an approach to managing and leading a team in any type of industry. Depending upon the activities or situation, each of the three areas identified by Adair should help a manager to perform well by encouraging team members to achieve targets, improve quality, increase productivity and sustain a high level of morale.

Adair identified three core management responsibilities:

- achieving a task
- managing a team
- managing individuals.

The model suggests that emphasis should be placed upon:

- developing a plan to achieve the **task**, identify resources needed and monitor performance against the plan
- develop the **team**, maintain discipline, resolve conflict and communicate desired standards of performance and behaviour
- develop team members as **individuals**, offer support, utilise their skills, give praise and offer training and development.

Given that leadership is part of the management process, it may be helpful for you to think about the leadership qualities you will need to get the best from your team. Below are some skills, attributes and areas of knowledge you can consider.

Skills	**Attributes**	**Knowledge**
• listening, writing, speaking • delivery and presentations • coping with stress • delegating tasks • influencing others • motivating others • planning work activities • controlling resources • coaching others • solving problems	• honesty • enthusiasm • being decisive • unbiased view • leading by example • creativity • flexible approach • being imaginative • being approachable	• systems and procedures • products or services provided • staff welfare policies • your team members' capabilities • your organisation's and team's objectives • team members' preferred roles • team members' skills • financial tools and budgets • performance management • problem-solving tools and methodologies

Of course, there will be other skills, attributes and areas of knowledge not identified in the lists above, perhaps because of the nature of the business you work in. If you can think of additional items, discuss them with your assessor.

2

BTEC Unit 1: 1.2, 1.3
Unit 2: 1.1

Task 1b

Respond to the tasks that follow, using workplace examples where possible.

1. I would describe the skills associated with leadership as:

2. Prepare a 250 word statement that clearly describes the differences between leadership and management.

3. Write a description of the knowledge and skills needed for effective management and leadership.

2. Functions of management

In 1917 French management theorist Henri Fayol identified five elements of the management function he considered to be important. Many organisations have since adopted these views, which are explored below.

1. To forecast and plan
Managers should plan for the future by setting business objectives and putting strategies in place to achieve those objectives. Policies and procedures should be devised that will help the organisation to meet its goals.

2. To organise
Managers should make the best use of resources (time, money, people, equipment and materials) and carefully examine how work is allocated in the organisation. There should be appropriate investment in training, clear direction for staff and clearly defined responsibilities.

3. To command
Instructions should be issued, tactfully, to staff in an effort to enhance performance. Careful decision-making activity is necessary, as is the responsibility of ensuring tasks are carried out correctly.

4. To coordinate
Managers must make sure objectives are met. All activities in the business should be coordinated in such a way that there is effective communication and regular exchange of information (for example, in meetings).

5. To control
Managers should measure the activities of individuals and teams to ensure that performance fits in with plans. This process includes inspection, quality control procedures and taking corrective action as necessary.

All businesses need to know what their aims and targets are for the future, both in the long- and short-term. Part of your role as a manager is helping to put together this plan.

2

BTEC Unit 1: 1.1
PLTS RL: 5
CT: 1, 3

PLTS

In this task you will need to evaluate your experiences and think creatively on how Henri Fayol's functions of management will assist you in managing.

Task 2

Examine Henri Fayol's five functions of management. Write a paragraph which explains how useful you think these functions will be when managing your own team. Use the space below.

3. Assessing your own leadership performance

Obtaining feedback on your performance as a manager can be very useful to enable you to identify areas where improvements might be required. A 360-degree appraisal process offers the opportunity to obtain feedback from many colleagues who work with you rather than just your own line manager.

It may be the case that your organisation does not operate a 360-degree appraisal system. Nevertheless, collecting information about your own performance can be very beneficial and can help you to build on your strengths as a manager and identify any areas that need some improvement.

Below is an example of a feedback form that could be adapted (if necessary) to gather information about your own performance.

Performance Assessment Questionnaire

As valued colleagues I would be grateful if you would spend a few minutes of your time to complete this questionnaire, which will inform me of your views on my workplace performance as a manager and leader of my team.

Please be as honest as you like, as I will use your feedback to assess my performance and to help me to update my personal development plan.

Please respond to each of the statements below, rating my performance as 1 excellent; 2 very good; 3 good; 4 fair; 5 poor.

Please give feedback on my performance as a manager by circling the rating you consider appropriate alongside each statement:

1. My technical knowledge	1	2	3	4	5
2. My ability to be supportive to others	1	2	3	4	5
3. My ability to communicate effectively	1	2	3	4	5
4. My ability to make informed decisions	1	2	3	4	5
5. Your view of my patience with others	1	2	3	4	5
6. My knowledge of workplace procedures	1	2	3	4	5
7. My ability to work as part of a team	1	2	3	4	5
8. Your view of how fairly I treat people	1	2	3	4	5
9. Your opinion of how trustworthy and honest I am	1	2	3	4	5
10. How do you rate my knowledge of my team members' skills?	1	2	3	4	5
11. My ability to motivate my team members	1	2	3	4	5
12. My ability to delegate tasks to others fairly	1	2	3	4	5
13. My ability to plan tasks to meet objectives	1	2	3	4	5
14. Your view on my ability to cope with stress	1	2	3	4	5
15. My ability to deliver oral presentations with confidence	1	2	3	4	5

Now please complete the details below:

Your name:

Position:

Date:

Signature:

2

Any other comments on my workplace performance:

____

____

____

____

____

Thank you for taking the time to complete this form.

Please return it to . . . . by . . . .

NVQ Unit 5: 4.1, 4.2

Task 3a

Using a feedback questionnaire similar to the one above, gather feedback from your colleagues and peers on your current performance. Design a form that you can use to capture feedback on how you perform from at least four of your colleagues. (These should include your line manager, two members of the team you lead, and a colleague from another department if possible. Please discuss this with your assessor.)

PLTS IE: 2, 3, 4, 6

> **PLTS**
> In completing this task, you will need to carry out some research, explore ideas and support your conclusions with reasoned arguments

Your feedback form should be designed in such a way that it captures the name and position of the person giving you the feedback. Remember to leave room for them to sign and date it.

Then, using the space below, analyse the information you have obtained and provide a brief summary of your findings.

BTEC Unit 2: 2.3

Task 3b

Analyse the ways in which you could use feedback obtained from others to improve your management and leadership performance.

4. Assessing your own career and personal goals

You are likely to have personal ambitions regarding what you would like to achieve throughout your career and also within your personal life. Being able to identify where you want your career path to take you will assist you to develop plans for your future.

There are three useful questions that you can give answers to, in order to develop a personal action plan to assist with planning your career path and personal goals:

1. Where am I now?
Make an assessment of the position you hold currently.

For example, *I currently work as a First Line Manager, overseeing the work of seven inbound call centre staff.*

2. Where do I want to be?
Decide what you would benefit from and would like to be doing in the next one to five years.

For example, *In one year, I want to enrol on a middle management training course, within two years I want to be managing a larger team of outbound call operations, and within five years I want to be overseeing several departments, working as a middle manager.*

3. How will I get there?
Decide on actions you will take to achieve your responses to question 2 above.

For example, *I will discuss an appropriate middle management course with HR and my line manager, I will apply for management positions with more responsibility, and I will continue to acquire experience / gain additional qualifications, as necessary, to work towards overseeing the work of several departments.*

Successful completion of a training course will give you a valuable record of achievement and demonstrate your desire to progress.

In effect, by working through the three-step process above you are setting objectives for yourself (where do I want to be?), and putting strategies in place to help you to achieve your personal objectives (how will I get there?).

SWOT analysis

A SWOT analysis is a useful tool which can be used to analyse strengths, weaknesses, opportunities and threats. The tool can be used at:

- **corporate level**: senior managers or directors can use it to help with planning and decision making at the top level of the organisation
- **departmental level**: departmental managers and their teams can use it to enhance performance (for example, by brainstorming ideas in team meetings)
- **individual level**: individuals can use the tool to help identify their personal goals. They can examine their strengths (which they can build upon), any weaknesses they may have (areas for improvement), the opportunities they may have for the future and any threats which may present themselves (any obstacles to prevent development).

2

Examine the example below:

SWOT analysis – personal career goals	
Strengths	**Weaknesses**
Communication skills Approachable Knowledgeable Technically minded Good time-keeping	Unassertive nature Poor negotiation skills Not good at dealing with conflict
Opportunities	**Threats**
Middle management training course Assertiveness training Conflict resolution training	Nervous at interviews Not willing to relocate Limited time to attend training sessions due to family commitments

NVQ Unit 5: 1.1
WorkSkills Unit 7: 1.1
PLTS RL: 1, 3, 5

Task 4a

Prepare a SWOT analysis to identify your strengths, weaknesses (areas for improvement), opportunities and threats, using the table below.

PLTS

task encourages self assessment, review of progress, evaluation of experiences and future opportunities

Strengths	**Weaknesses**
Opportunities	**Threats**

WorkSkills Unit 7: 1.3

Task 4b

a. How will you manage the threats identified in your SWOT analysis?

2

b. One of your threats or risks could be lack of time to complete learning due to work and family commitments. How would you overcome this?

Note: A SWOT analysis should, ideally, always be followed up with an action plan, so that you and your managers can identify clear actions to help you achieve the personal goals and objectives you have set as a result of your analysis. An example Action plan template is provided below.

Name:						
Job title:				**Date:**		
Action/task	**By whom**	**By when**	**Resources needed**	**Completion date**	**Review date**	**Manager signature**
Obtain information and enrol upon a middle management training course	myself	30 May 2013	time fees materials information	31 July 2013	28 Nov 2013	
Organise shadowing of an experienced production manager	myself HR line manager	30 June 2013	time	30 June 2013	30 Sept 2013	
Organise job rotation with other manager	myself	21 July 2013	time	22 July 2013	25 Aug 2013	
Implement coaching sessions from experienced production manager	myself line manager HR a production manager	30 June 2013	learning style inventory training plan time review sheets	30 June 2013	30 Nov 2013	

Using SMART objectives

When setting your personal objectives, you may find it helpful to use the acronym SMART. In other words the objectives you set should be:

- Specific
- Measurable
- Achievable
- Realistic
- Time-bound.

Using SMART objectives offers a more meaningful approach to your planning activity. For example, if one of your objectives is 'To work towards being a middle manager', there is little description of your intentions to achieve it. If, however, you rewrite your objective as 'To enrol upon a CIM Level 4 Middle Management training programme, to help to work towards middle management status by 31 March 2013', then there is a greater focus of how you intend to achieve your objective, and by when!

It is useful to consider that your personal work-related SMART objectives should be agreed with your line manager and should, in some way, assist your team and your organisation to achieve their own SMART business objectives.

Everyone's individual SMART objectives (often identified during staff appraisals) should link to the organisation's SMART objectives. With everyone working together to help the organisation to meet its objectives, jobs are more likely to remain secure and this, in turn, highlights the importance of every individual's personal development within an organisation.

5. Developing a plan for further development

Feedback from others, and activities you have undertaken, such as your SWOT analysis and discussions you have had with your line manager, perhaps as the result of your staff appraisal, may have provided you with the opportunity to produce a plan to develop your knowledge and skills further.

As part of your planning process, you may find it useful to devise a table similar to the one below:

Identified opportunities for development	Skills/knowledge gap	SMART objectives	Resources needed and/or support from others	Training opportunities
To be more effective and efficient with time management to reduce stress	Need to address ability to manage time effectively and efficiently	To successfully complete a time management course, by 30 June 2013	Staff time Training materials Training budget Transport costs Support from line managers	One-day course at local college's Business School

It is always a good idea not to set too many personal objectives at any one time. This can be overwhelming, and you may become de-motivated! It can, however, be useful to identify personal objectives you would like to meet in the future.

Skills audit

A skills audit is a process of identifying skills gaps. By completing a skills audit, you will be able to identify your training needs.

A skills audit will:

- identify the skills required currently and for the future
- provide a targeted analysis of your development needs.

A simple skills audit table has been given below:

Skill	**Currently possess? (Y/N)**	**Will I need this skill to meet my personal objective? (Y/N)**
Problem-solving skills		
Delivery of effective oral presentations		
Control of resources		

Remember: to achieve your personal objectives you will need to be fully aware of your existing skills, knowledge and attributes, and you may already have identified a gap between those that you currently possess and those that you will need for future development.

Once you have identified the skills you need to be an effective manager, you will need advice and guidance. There are also a number of people within your organisation whom you could contact for support. For example:

- line manager
- human resources manager
- mentor
- training officer.

There are a number of organisations and departments you can contact, who will advise and guide you about the best way forward. For example:

- local colleges and universities
- sector-specific authorities
- local authority
- professional bodies (for example, awarding bodies such as Edexcel)
- Citizens Advice Bureau.

In the space below, identify the sources of information necessary to enable you to progress with your career path.

WorkSkills Unit 9: 4.1, 4.2

Task 5

Describe in the space below the occupational opportunities that are available within your sector.

Describe in the space below the occupational opportunities that are available within other related sectors.

A Personal Development Plan (PDP) will enable you to identify the skills you need to gain and the actions you will need to take to develop these skills. Your plan needs to be agreed with your line manager and will usually be drawn up as part of your staff appraisal process.

2

Your plan should help you to identify:

- what you want to learn
- the skills you wish to develop
- the actions you need to take – and by when
- the resources you will need
- the support you will need
- when you will review the progress you have made.

Below is an example of a Personal Development Plan:

Personal Development Plan				
Name of post holder: **Date of today's review:** **Date of last review:**		**Name of manager:**		
What skills/ knowledge do I need/want to develop?	**What actions must I take to achieve this?**	**What resources and/or support will I need?**	**Target date for completion**	**Target date for review with manager**
Development objective 1 *Managing time effectively and efficiently*	*Attend an external college course*	*Time to attend, fees and support from manager*	*30 June 2013*	*30 July 2013*
Development objective 2				
Development objective 3				
Post holder's signature:		**Manager's signature:**		

EVIDENCE GATHERING

NVQ Unit 1: 1.1, 1.2, 2.1, 3.1, 3.2
Unit 5: 4.1, 4.2
WorkSkills Unit 7: 1.2, 1.4, 1.6, 2.1, 2.3, 2.4
Unit 9: 4.3

Managing your own professional development

In this next activity, you will gather evidence from your workplace to show you can manage your own professional development.

The evidence you have to present will need to show how you assess your own career and personal goals, set your own personal work objectives, produce a development plan and monitor and review this plan with your manager. Examples of possible evidence that you may consider for this purpose are:

- a recently completed personal development plan, including work and personal goals
- examples of feedback from colleagues and managers (for example, employee of the week, emails)
- copies of certificates of training attained and completed
- a previous PDP to show how development has taken place
- training plans
- action plan to show how you intend to meet your development needs
- one-to-one supervision documentation showing reflection
- reflective account – reflecting upon how useful training was to assist with achieving career and personal goals.

In addition to the above evidence, your manager may need to write a witness testimony that describes how you agree your SMART objectives, and how you monitor and review your development plan.

PUTTING IT INTO PRACTICE

NVQ Unit 1: 1.1, 1.2, 2.1, 3.1, 4.2
WorkSkills Unit 7: 1.1, 1.2, 1.3, 1.4, 1.6, 2.1, 2.3, 2.4

Observation of an appraisal and/or discussion with manager to agree a training plan

At this stage of this set of activities, it may be necessary for your assessor to observe a PDR (professional development review) meeting between you and your manager in order to assess how you discuss and set your goals, agree SMART objectives and reflect upon the outcomes of the learning experience.

It will be necessary for you and your assessor to negotiate and agree a suitable time and date with your manager to carry out this observation. In addition, your assessor will refer to a checklist during the observation in order to ensure that as many of the criteria as possible are covered.

PROFESSIONAL DISCUSSION

BTEC Unit 1: 1.3
Unit 2: 2.1, 2.2, 3.1, 3.2, 3.3, 3.4
NVQ Unit 1: 1.1, 1.2, 2.1, 3.1, 3.2, 4.1, 4.2
Unit 5: 1.2, 4.1, 4.2
WorkSkills Unit 7: 2.2, 2.3

Once you have gathered your workplace evidence and your assessor has observed you taking part in a professional development review (PDR) with your manager, the next stage is for your assessor to conduct a professional discussion. The purpose of this discussion is to check your competency at this level of knowledge and understanding for this topic area.

It will be necessary for you to prepare for this discussion and below are some topic areas you should consider. In addition, you will need to provide workplace examples relating to the following:

- how to produce a plan using a skills audit
- the staff appraisal process
- the importance of identifying and assessing your own career and personal goals
- techniques used to obtain feedback from colleagues, peers and managers
- the importance of obtaining feedback on your performance as a leader
- evaluate your strengths within your own area of responsibility
- factors you need to take into consideration when setting SMART objectives
- explain how you would set SMART learning goals so that you can complete your learning on time and to a high standard and manage both work and personal life commitments
- explanation of the components of a development plan and its purpose
- techniques you will use to monitor and review your personal development plan
- the resources and activities available to you to complete a PDP
- why it is important to revise learning goals in response to any training that has taken place.

Your assessor will advise you on what will need to be discussed in detail during the professional discussion meeting. Your assessor may use a digital recorder to record your discussion and questioning process. This recording will then be used as evidence to show your competency in the criteria identified.

Discussion process

In addition to the professional discussion, your assessor may ask you questions during or at the end of the discussion in order to give you the opportunity to demonstrate your understanding of managing your own professional development and improving your management and leadership performance. To prepare for the questions posed, you will need to think about how you could answer questions such as the following:

- What is the difference between management and leadership?
- What are the benefits of obtaining feedback from colleagues, peers and managers?
- What will you do with this information?
- Give examples, by referring to the evidence presented earlier, of how you have made changes in response to feedback received from others.
- What is a skills audit?

In order for you and your team to meet targets, you will need to plan your tasks and activities carefully.

In this section you will find a range of activities to help you prepare and gather evidence for your assessment in relation to:

1. Enhancing the performance of your team

Your team's ability to meet its targets will, in turn, have an impact upon your organisation's ability to achieve its business objectives. If these are not met it may lead to unhappy customers and possible lost business.

You must take into account that your team needs direction and it is important for you to communicate objectives to your team with clarity. You will also need to monitor your team's performance effectively and evaluate progress made.

It may be necessary for your assessor to visit you at your workplace to observe you carrying out a staff appraisal and/or participating in a team meeting. Your assessor will take notes during the observations and this record will then provide evidence for your portfolio. Because confidentiality is important, it will be necessary for you to check with your team members that they have no objections to observations or recordings taking place while they are in the presence of your assessor.

3

1. ENHANCING THE PERFORMANCE OF YOUR TEAM

KNOWLEDGE AND UNDERSTANDING

1. Setting objectives

When planning work activities and setting objectives, managers often refer to the acronym SMART. This should ensure that objectives are:

- Specific
- Measurable
- Achievable
- Realistic
- Time-bound.

Without applying SMART criteria, a departmental or team objective might read, for example, as 'To reduce the rate of accidents in the department'. If SMART criteria are applied, the same objective might read as 'To reduce the incidence of hand injuries to operatives in the production department by 50% by 31 December 2013'.

Managers would then need to devise strategies and put these in place to ensure the objective is met.

Consider what the outcomes might be if you didn't take steps to:

1. agree your team's SMART objectives with your team members
2. communicate your team's SMART objectives to your team members
3. ensure your team's SMART objectives align with your organisation's SMART business objectives
4. set SMART personal work objectives with team members
5. set yourself SMART objectives to help you to manage your own area of responsibility.

BTEC Unit 1: 4.1
NVQ Unit 2: 1.2
Unit 5: 2.2

Task 1

Examine each of the statements in the numbered list above, and write a response to each of them, indicating your views of likely outcomes if they are not addressed.

1.

2.

3.

4.

5.

Involving your team in the planning process

By involving your team members in the planning of the work you are likely to:

- improve levels of morale and motivation
- provide clarity and a focus for team members
- be able to agree upon priorities and responsibilities
- obtain feedback quickly from team members.

It needs to be clear that final decisions rest with you as manager, but involving your team members in decision making and planning will show that you respect and trust their views. This can help to encourage a culture of achievement within which SMART objectives are more likely to be achieved.

The planning process will require you to be aware of:

- the tasks that may motivate or de-motivate those who possess certain skills
- the tasks that have to be done and by when
- the number of team members who are available
- the mix of skills, specialisms or experiences among your team members
- the resources available to enable you to successfully complete the task, such as sufficient equipment and materials.

3

Involving team members in the planning process can improve morale, motivation and performance.

Remember: When planning tasks and activities it is a good idea to devise contingency plans in anticipation of delays or interruptions. A contingency can be defined as 'something that may or may not happen', and a contingency plan means having a back-up idea should something go wrong. In a hospital, for example, if a power cut occurs, a plan is in place for an emergency generator to operate immediately.

BTEC Unit 1: 4.1
NVQ Unit 2: 1.2

Task 2

Spend some time thinking about how you might agree your SMART work objectives with your team members. Produce a 500-word document that describes the value of doing this with.

2. Supporting and guiding staff

Your team members need to understand exactly what their work objectives are trying to achieve and what their part in this is. If you agree SMART objectives with your team members, they are more likely to take ownership of the tasks and actions needed to achieve them. The level of support you offer your team members can serve to influence the achievement of your team's objectives. There are many ways you can provide support, which may include:

- team meetings, briefings and debriefings
- coaching, mentoring and buddying
- offering constructive feedback
- giving praise, when appropriate
- arranging training and responding to development requests
- ensuring your team has sufficient resources to carry out tasks
- one-to-one review meetings
- arranging flexible working conditions.

Offering support can help to increase levels of morale and motivation, helping your team to achieve their objectives.

3

BTEC Unit 1: 4.2

Task 3

Complete the table below to help you compare ways of providing support that will help your team to meet its objectives. Select three methods from the list above. (An example has been done for you.)

Method of support	Advantages	Disadvantages
Arranging training for a team member	*Gives team members new skills, raising their self-esteem and morale.* *Helps performance of team.*	*Can be costly and use up the training budget.* *Takes team members away from their jobs while training so cover will need to be arranged.*

BTEC Unit 1: 4.2

Task 4

Using the table below, identify three techniques you currently use to support your team members in meeting their work objectives. Compare how effective they are. (One example has been done.)

Support technique	Its effectiveness
Team meetings	*Allows me to give team feedback and group support. But there is no one-to-one time to discuss individual problems or concerns.*

PLTS RL: 1

PLTS

This task will allow you to demonstrate your reflective learning skills. You will need to assess supporting techniques and evaluate their effectiveness.

The importance of promoting quality in the workplace

The success of your organisation largely depends upon the quality of the product or service it provides. Poor quality is likely to result in:

- unhappy customers
- a poor image and reputation
- additional costs due to the need to redo work
- increased waste (materials and other resources)
- delays in processing customer orders.

Your organisation may use quality processes such as Total Quality Management (TQM) or perhaps it may be ISO 9000 registered. Whichever quality assurance process is used, managers at all levels need to show that they are committed to it and fully support it. This will help to develop a culture of quality in the workplace.

Having a 'culture of quality' means that quality becomes everyone's responsibility, with everyone working towards the same quality standards within your organisation. Ways to promote and develop a culture of quality include:

- quality circles – teams are given time to hold meetings to discuss how they can improve quality
- self-managed teams – everyone in the team works at the same level, monitoring their own tasks and sharing out responsibilities with no obvious leader present for most of their shift
- acting upon feedback – procedures and the way things are done may be changed as a result of feedback from customer surveys or other stakeholders
- examining ways to improve communication – the way messages and information are sent may need to be improved (for example, to colleagues, customers and suppliers) and the way feedback is obtained and acted upon may need to be addressed.

Remember: Ensuring your team members read all of your organisation's policies and procedures will help to ensure everyone works to the same standards of quality. It's always a good idea to get your team members to sign to say that they have read and understood the content of these documents.

BTEC Unit 1: 5.1

Task 5

How can obtaining feedback from your customers be used to develop a quality culture in your organisation?

Sometimes obstacles may present themselves that can make it more difficult for you to promote quality in your organisation. These barriers may include:

- lack of commitment from senior managers
- badly written procedures and policies
- poorly structured staff appraisals and one-to-one meetings
- the organisation's business objectives not being shared with everyone
- poor and ineffective communication between departments and individuals
- inadequate training and development for staff members.

BTEC Unit 1: 5.2

Task 6

Design an information leaflet that you can share with other managers entitled 'Potential barriers to promoting quality in the workplace'. Your leaflet should be one side of A4 and should use small paragraphs and bullet lists to describe possible barriers to promoting quality in the workplace.

3. Conducting staff appraisals

Staff appraisals exist to appraise the performance of employees and identify their future development needs. When you conduct staff appraisals with your team members, you will need to discuss their strengths and weaknesses, identify their progress and achievements and set SMART objectives for their future development.

Conducting staff appraisals effectively will help to ensure you have a motivated and productive team. This in turn means your team is more likely to meet its targets, to work to agreed standards or quality, to help your organisation to achieve its objectives, and to satisfy your customers' needs. You should consider how the development of your team members helps your team to achieve its targets and your organisation to achieve its business objectives.

When conducting a staff appraisal you should:

- explain the purpose and format of the appraisal process to your appraisee from the outset
- encourage your appraisee to fully contribute
- make sure you have the appropriate documentation to use, that is in line with your organisation's requirements
- make sure that trust and rapport are developed throughout the appraisal
- make sure that listening, questioning and summarising are carried out effectively
- review achievements and progress made by the appraisee
- agree future training and development needs with your appraisee.

Remember: Authorisation may be needed from your own manager or your Human Resources department.

Before the staff appraisal meeting it is important for you (the appraiser) and your team member (the appraisee) to prepare yourselves well. For you as the appraiser, this will include:

- making sure others know you must not be disturbed
- confirming the booking of a quiet, warm and comfortable room
- agreeing your 'agenda' with your appraisee beforehand
- checking over your appraisal documentation (Are you familiar with it? Do you have all necessary forms – including action plans from previous appraisals, if appropriate?)
- ensuring you have a copy of your appraisee's job description and performance standards
- producing a list of relevant open questions you wish to ask, that are designed to promote discussion.

A staff appraisal helps employees to judge their progress and identify areas where they may wish to gain more experience or training.

For your appraisee, this preparation will include:

- putting together documentation that will include his or her job description, a list of current duties and, if appropriate, the action plan from the previous appraisal
- collating evidence of training/qualifications (for example, certificates)
- collating evidence of targets and standards that have been met
- producing a statement of training and development needs that can be requested and discussed
- producing a list of questions to be asked.

Remember: Your Human Resources department may issue standard documentation which you and your appraisee are expected to complete prior to and during the appraisal interview.

BTEC Unit 5: 1.1, 1.2

Task 7

Produce a short statement (about 250 words) briefly describing:

1. the purpose of appraisals as a tool to develop your team members

2. the value of you and your appraisee preparing yourselves prior to the appraisal.

BTEC Unit 5: 1.3

Task 8

Using the table below, compare the value of different interview techniques in appraisal interviews.

Interview techniques	Advantages	Disadvantages
1. Keeping to the point	*Prevents the interview from running over time*	*May cause the appraisee to think he/she cannot have sufficient time to expand their answers*
2. Eye contact		
3. Asking open questions		
4. Being diplomatic		
5. Time management		

4. Evaluating work performance

Only by taking the time to carry out an evaluation will you know if your performance targets – and those of your team – are being met. You can do this by:

- checking if SMART objectives, targets and key performance indicators (KPIs) have been met
- examining absenteeism within your team
- conducting staff appraisals with your team members
- identifying the reasons for any internal or external customer complaints
- examining the reasons for any re-working of products, wastage or quality rejects
- checking to see if you are working within budget (you may need to consult your line manager in order to do this).

When evaluating performance you should take into account that some of the data you have sourced, such as KPIs or number of complaints, may be inaccurate or insufficient and that this might prevent a professional judgement from being made. You may need to revisit your source if this is the case. Feedback from colleagues, customers and suppliers can be a useful source of performance evaluation, but you should be aware of the following common pitfalls:

- Halo effect – a person is rated highly on face value by those offering feedback but generally does not perform well in work
- Horns effect – a person is given negative feedback because of one error, when they usually do perform well in work.

Some organisations operate a 360-degree feedback system. This enables feedback on performance to be sought from other colleagues in your organisation rather than just your line manager and your Human Resources department. The feedback received should inform you about your performance, skills level, working relationships, management style and approachability.

3

BTEC Unit 1: 2.1

Task 9a

Produce a short statement, approximately 150 words in length, that describes the methods that can be used to allocate work to your team members.

BTEC Unit 5: 2.1
PLTS CT: 1

PLTS

npleting this task, you will generate ideas and explore possibilities on work performance.

Task 9b

Write a brief statement (approximately 250–300 words) that compares methods of measuring work performance.

3

BTEC Unit 5: 2.2, 2.3

Task 10

Now respond to the two statements below:

1. Describe three common pitfalls when evaluating workplace performance.

2. Analyse the merits of your organisation providing 360-degree feedback.

5. Development of objectives

Your team members are likely to share a combination of learning styles. This means some of your team members will prefer to learn through a 'hands on' approach and getting involved with a task, whereas others may prefer to observe and reflect on a task (perhaps by watching a demonstration) before they undertake it.

Educational theorists, such as Honey and Mumford or Kolb, have carried out research into learning styles and some have produced questionnaires that can assess and evaluate the preferred learning style of a person. Before organising and setting learning and development objectives for your team members (perhaps as a result of the outcomes of their staff appraisal), you may find it helpful to evaluate their preferred learning styles.

BTEC Unit 5: 3.1

Task 11

Carry out some research to find out about:

1. Kolb's experiential learning model

2. Honey and Mumford's model.

Prepare a 250-word statement outlining the key points from your research. You should describe the links between learning styles and appropriate methods of learning.

Setting development objectives for your team members can:

- improve motivation and levels of morale
- provide direction and focus
- prioritise activities and tasks
- improve decision making
- encourage mutual trust, understanding and personal growth.

3

Remember: Agreeing development objectives with your team members requires you to ensure that the objectives are SMART. If, for example, they are not achievable this will de-motivate your team members.

BTEC Unit 5: 3.2

Task 12

Reflect upon how you set out learning and developing objectives for your team members. Outline the methods you would use to set these objectives

Discuss your answers with your assessor.

You may find some of your team members resist any change you wish to introduce. For example, to ensure your team achieves its targets and your organisation achieves its business objectives, it may be necessary for you, from time to time, to introduce new ways of working. This may, in turn, require you to agree and decide on new development objectives for your team members. Some of them may resist the changes to their working patterns, perhaps due to fear of not being able to carry out their new role.

BTEC Unit 5: 3.3

Task 13

Spend some time carrying out some research into 'change management'. Describe some methods of overcoming resistance to change. Prepare a 500-word document outlining your findings.

EVIDENCE GATHERING

In this activity you will identify an area of your work that will capture evidence of how you operate as a team leader. Your assessor will help you to identify suitable items of evidence.

NVQ Unit 2: 1.1, 1.2, 1.3, 2.1, 2.3
Unit 5: 2.1, 2.2, 3.1, 3.2

a. How you will communicate the purpose and objectives of the team to all team members

Suggested evidence may include:

1. minutes of meetings where you are:

- discussing the purpose of the team and agreeing/negotiating team objectives
- communicating the purpose and objectives of the team
- negotiating and agreeing SMART team objectives that align with those of the organisation
- discussing how team objectives will be achieved
- developing plans to assist the team to achieve their objectives
- obtaining feedback from colleagues and team in order to revisit and amend plans

3

2. emails:
   - reminding team of their tasks and objectives
   - offering support and guidance
3. daily/weekly/monthly reports:
   - outlining their targets for the day/week/month
4. action plans:
   - identifying the team's responsibilities and deadlines for completing these tasks.

BTEC Unit 5: 3.2
NVQ Unit 2: 3.1, 3.2, 3.3, 3.4, 4.1, 4.2
Unit 5: 2.2, 3.1
Unit 18: 2.1, 2.2, 3.1, 3.2, 3.3

b. Staff appraisal documentation as completed with a team member

Suggested evidence may include:

1. evidence in the appraisal documentation of:
   - identifying opportunities and difficulties faced by the individual and identifying techniques to manage these
   - providing support and advice to overcome these difficulties and challenges
   - supporting and providing advice on how the individual can make the most out of the opportunities available to them
   - monitoring and reviewing their progress
   - giving recognition to the individual for work done and objectives achieved
2. action plans/training plans/development plans
3. own meeting notes taken during a meeting with a member of staff to address performance problems
4. confidential records taken in line with the disciplinary procedures

Minutes are an important record of meetings and can be valuable evidence of your contribution and achievements.

Note: Please make sure you either obtain the permission of the staff member and manager before showing the documentation to your assessor, or remove all confidential information from the documentation such as name, address, staff number and so on, in order to comply with the Data Protection Act.

5. organisational policies and/or procedures (for example, disciplinary procedures)
6. examples of emails sent to a staff member outlining performance problems.

NVQ Unit 2: 3.1, 3.2, 3.3, 3.4, 4.2
Workskills Unit 7: 1.5

c. Supporting your team members

Suggested evidence may include:

1. email examples of you responding and offering support to team members who are facing difficult issues
2. email examples providing feedback to individual team members on work completed
3. 'Employee of the Month' certificates given to employees
4. one-to-one/supervision documentation:
   - outlining problems and/or challenges faced and how to overcome these
   - providing support and advice on how to complete tasks
5. brainstorming sessions as a group to encourage teamwork.

PUTTING IT INTO PRACTICE

This activity will enable your assessor to examine your competence by observing you carrying out workplace activities. This might include asking related questions to test your underpinning knowledge.

NVQ Unit 2: 2.2, 4.1, 4.2
Unit 5: 2.1, 2.2
WorkSkills Unit 6: 1.1, 1.2, 1.3, 1.4, 1.5, 2.1, 2.2

a. Observation of a team/management meeting

During this meeting, the assessor will be observing your ability to:

- discuss complex tasks with the team
- negotiate with other staff, i.e. not your team (for example, your manager, line manager, colleagues from different departments) complex tasks for your team to take on which have a local focus
- lead discussions with either your team or other staff to agree plans for completing a specific task
- lead a team

3

PLTS TW: 1, 2, 4, 6
IE: 1, 3, 4

PLTS

During the team meeting you will have the opportunity to discuss common goals with your team members and reach agreements. You will need to allow all members to take part and contribute in this meeting and you will need to show fairness and consideration to all. During the discussions you will need to answer questions and resolve problems, explore events or problems as expressed by various individuals, and analyse and evaluate information to make an informed decision.

BTEC Unit 5: 1.1, 2.1, 3.2
NVQ Unit 2: 1.2, 1.3, 2.1, 2.4
Unit 5: 3.2
Unit 18: 1.1, 3.1, 3.2, 3.3, 4.1, 4.2, 4.3

- revisit plans and revise and/or amend them to ensure deadlines are met
- recap current plans and review whether targets have been achieved
- encourage team members to participate in discussions
- encourage team members to think creatively about any issues or challenges they may be experiencing
- monitor and review the progress of the team
- give recognition to individuals and the team for work completed and objectives achieved
- implement objectives with colleagues and team members.

b. Observation of a staff appraisal meeting with an individual who is underperforming

Before this observation can take place, it will be necessary for you to check with the member of staff that is it reasonable for your assessor to attend the meeting. Also, it will be necessary for you to check with your manager that this is acceptable.

During this staff appraisal meeting, your assessor will be observing your ability to:

- explain the importance of conducting a staff appraisal
- communicate the team's purpose and objectives
- discuss the team member's role and their contribution needed to achieve the team's objectives
- measure work performance
- set SMART personal work objectives with the team member
- set individual objectives in line with the team's objectives
- gather feedback from colleagues prior to the meeting and discuss this with your team member
- communicate the organisation's policies in relation to managing performance problems
- provide detailed feedback on the team member's performance
- discuss reasons for underperforming
- identify courses of action to manage this
- discuss and explain the course of action needed as a result of the underperformance
- explain any legal requirements, industry regulations, organisational policies and professional codes relating to the job role

PLTS EP: 1, 2, 3, 4, 5

PLTS

By carrying out a staff appraisal you will be given the opportunity to demonstrate your Effective Participator skills. You will be discussing areas of concern, suggesting improvements that will help the staff member as well as the team and put forward a persuasive case for action.

- discuss and agree on a detailed development plan to deal with change
- offer support, advice and guidance
- take notes in order to keep a confidential record of the discussion that has taken place
- review and revise any confidential records taken previously.

BTEC Unit 1: 2.3, 4.2
Unit 5: 1.1
NVQ Unit 2: 1.1, 1.2, 1.3, 2.1, 2.2, 2.3, 2.4, 3.1, 3.2, 3.3, 3.4, 4.2
Unit 18: 2.1, 2.2, 3.3, 4.1, 4.2, 4.3
WorkSkills Unit 6: 1.1, 1.3, 2.1, 2.2, 2.3
Unit 7: 1.5

PROFESSIONAL DISCUSSION

Your assessor will conduct a professional discussion with you, which will capture evidence necessary to prove your level of knowledge and understanding of topic areas.

Below are some topic areas you will need to consider when preparing for the professional discussion with your assessor:

- the purpose and objectives of your team
- the importance of ensuring all team members are aware of their purpose and objectives
- how team meetings can be used to:
  - help set team plans and objectives
  - provide support and advice
  - manage difficulties and challenges
  - recognise work achieved/completed
- how a staff appraisal meeting can be used to set objectives and provide support
- how an appraisal can be used as a tool to develop staff
- techniques you use to communicate the purpose and objectives of your team
- how you monitor and review completed work
- the importance of getting your team to think creatively
- how you support your team members when faced with difficulties and challenges
- how you manage a team member who is underperforming
- the importance of negotiating with other staff complex issues that have a local focus
- how to assess the performance of your team and the importance of doing so
- how you would analyse the links between the skills you have as a leader and the motivation of your team members
- how to identify suitable actions to deal with identified problems
- techniques used to identify performance problems
- the importance of reviewing and revising confidential records with team members

3

PLTS IE: 2, 6

PLTS

Your assessor will use a digital recorder to record your professional discussion and the questioning process. This recording will then be used as a piece of evidence to prove your competence in the criteria identified under each section. You may need to carry out some research in preparation to the discussion, and will need to make sure you have evidence to support your arguments.

NVQ Unit 2: 1.2
Unit 18: 1.1, 1.2, 2.2, 3.3
WorkSkills Unit 6: 2.2, 2.3

- techniques you use to lead a team to complete a task on time
- the importance of evaluating the success of the team
- how your team is structured (for example, leader, shapers, followers)
- motivation techniques you use.

Your assessor will plan the content of your professional discussion and will advise you in order to help you to prepare beforehand. The professional discussion may cover more than this section of your Workbook.

Discussion process

The questioning process will offer you the opportunity to demonstrate your knowledge and understanding further in setting objectives with your team, planning and putting strategies in place to achieve the objectives, and understanding the importance of the individual team roles.

To prepare for your professional discussion, you should think about how you could answer questions such as the following:

- What are SMART objectives?
- If you were unable to deal with an underperforming team member, what would you do?
- What are the legal requirements and industry regulations you must be aware of when dealing with a member of staff who is not meeting the quality standards (i.e. underperforming)?
- What are the organisation's policies and professional codes that you must be aware of when managing and supporting an underperforming member of staff?
- Give examples of why team members are not meeting their targets.
- Why is it important to keep confidential records of any discussions that have taken place regarding underperformance?
- How do you ensure your team achieves its objectives on time and to the required standard?
- Why is it important to revisit and revise plans on a regular basis?
- How do you provide constructive feedback to your team?
- Why is it important to identify the roles of individuals in the team (for example, finisher, plant, team worker and so on)?

4

The reputation and success of your organisation depends upon its ability to offer your customers a positive experience from the time they make an enquiry or place an order, through to the time they receive their product or service.

In this section you will find a range of activities to help you prepare and gather evidence for your assessment in relation to the following topics:

1. Communicating customer service standards
2. Supporting your team in meeting customer service standards
3. Monitoring and evaluating customer service performance, systems and processes

It is important to build relationships with both your internal and external customers and, wherever possible, exceed their expectations.

Ask yourself how many times you have visited a business organisation and received poor customer service. If you have experienced this, it is likely that you have a negative view of the organisation as a whole, rather than the one or two individuals you dealt with. In other words, it may take just one member of staff to damage the image and reputation of your whole organisation.

It is important for everyone in your organisation to be customer-focused and to realise that without your customers, you won't have a business, and that ultimately job security may be threatened.

4

1. COMMUNICATING CUSTOMER SERVICE STANDARDS

KNOWLEDGE AND UNDERSTANDING

Customer service should be about reacting to your customers' changing expectations and trying to get things right first time.

The Institute of Customer Service is a professional body made up of members who may be registered as organisations or individuals. In addition, a networking organisation called the Customer Service Network exists, enabling members to share ideas and best practice relating to customer service.

BTEC Unit 3: 1.1

Task 1

1. Carry out some research into the work of the Institute of Customer Service and find out their definition of customer service.

2. Having carried out your research, complete the sentence below by writing in the Institute's definition:

Customer Service is

____

____

Good customer service is about:

- providing a consistent and reliable service
- exceeding your customers' expectations

Listening well to your customers queries will help you to provide a consistent and reliable service.

- having a comprehensive knowledge of the goods or services you provide
- being honest with your customers (for example, about delays)
- providing accurate information
- communicating effectively, by getting the right message to the right people at the right time
- showing empathy and understanding (for example, when there is a complaint)
- listening well to your customers' queries and concerns
- providing a friendly and personal service.

Remember: You should treat your internal customers (your colleagues in your organisation) with the same respect and courtesy you would give your external customers.

BTEC Unit 3: 1.2

Task 2

Select four statements from the bullet list above that you consider to be the most important elements of providing good customer service. Give reasons for your responses. (An example has been done for you.)

Most important elements	Reasons why
Providing a friendly and personal service	*The customers will know that your organisation is approachable and that they can ask any questions without feeling embarrassed, and they will therefore return.*

4

Managing customer service delivery

Depending upon the nature of your business you may have:

- customers who make a one-off transaction and may not need to repeat their purchase in the short term (an example could be the purchase of a conservatory or a car)
- customers who make regular purchases, with whom you can build up a positive working relationship
- a combination of both.

It is important to consider that even customers who make a one-off purchase need to receive the same level of exceptional service as those who buy goods or services from you regularly.

These customers will talk to their family, friends and workplace colleagues about their experiences with your organisation and – if they have been treated in the right way – may persuade others to obtain goods or services from your organisation.

Even if you, your team members and others in your organisation are very customer-focused and provide an excellent service, it is still unwise to become complacent. Sometimes, if things are being done well, there can be a tendency to concentrate efforts on other aspects of business activity, to the detriment of the customer.

There should always be an approach to managing, reviewing and improving:

- systems and procedures currently in place (for example, complaints procedures)
- feedback from internal and external customers

Being approachable and customer focused will ensure you provide an excellent service.

- the retaining of existing customers and the gaining of new ones
- the quality of service given to customers
- communication between you and your colleagues in your own team and in other departments
- the accessibility and provision of accurate information
- customer service training for your team members
- adhering to relevant consumer legislation
- the monitoring of morale and motivation of your team members (as unhappy staff are not likely to offer exceptional customer service)
- how well each of your own team members accepts the importance of their role in providing customer service.

BTEC Unit 3: 1.2

Task 3a

PLTS IE: 1, 2, 3, 4, 5, 6
CT: 1, 2, 3
SM: 3

PLTS

By completing this task you will be demonstrating your Independent Enquirer, Creative Thinker and Self-Manager skills. You will need to communicate with your manager and colleagues to obtain their views and carry out your own research to respond to the statement given.

Produce an information leaflet (approximately one side of A4) entitled 'Ways of managing the delivery of customer service' that you could share with your team members. The content of your leaflet should offer a description of various ways that the delivery of customer service can be managed.

A combination of some research activity, your own ideas and responses obtained by talking to colleagues should help you.

Your assessor will negotiate a suitable deadline for this work to be done by.

Being aware of how legislation affects customer service delivery

You and your team members need to have an understanding of how consumer laws and regulations may impact upon the service you offer your customers.

Often, managers are so busy in organisations that there seems little time to make sure laws and regulations are being adhered to, let alone share these with team members. The courts, however, have little sympathy with organisations and their managers who do not operate in the best interests of their customers. In fact, the courts have a view that 'ignorance is no excuse'.

You need to have awareness and some understanding of your customers' statutory rights. While you are not expected to be a lawyer, having some familiarity with these laws and regulations can help to protect you from breaking the law.

4

Before you can share legal information with your team members, you need to be confident that you have some understanding of:

- the laws that directly affect your customers
- the laws that may indirectly affect your customers (for example, the Health and Safety at Work Act 1974 and the Data Protection Act 1998)
- what you and your team may be legally liable for and held accountable for.

BTEC Unit 3: 2.2
NVQ Unit 40: 1.1

Task 3b

Spend some time researching the following laws put in place by the Government to offer protection to consumers. These are often referred to as statutes (or Acts of Parliament).

Title of Statute	Protection/guarantees to consumers
The Sale of Goods Act 1979 (sections 12–15)	
The Trade Descriptions Act 1968	
The Consumer Protection Act 1987	
The Supply of Goods and Services Act 1982	
Distance Selling Regulations 2000	

You may also benefit from obtaining an understanding of the Unfair Contract Terms Act 1977, which states: 'no one may exclude or restrict liability for death or personal injury resulting from negligence by any contract term or notice'.

4

BTEC Unit 3: 2.2

Task 3c

Spend some time researching into the leading case Donaghue v Stevenson (1932), which relates to product liability and negligence.

Prepare a 250-word document outlining your findings.

EVIDENCE GATHERING

In this activity you will identify an area of your work that will capture evidence of how you operate as a team leader. Your assessor will help you to identify suitable items of evidence.

BTEC Unit 3: 1.1, 1.2, 2.2
NVQ Unit 40: 1.1, 1.2, 1.3

Communicating the customer service standards in your area of responsibility

You need to gather evidence of activity within areas of your work to demonstrate your ability to do this. Suggested evidence may include:

1. minutes of meetings where you communicate the following:
   - organisational policies and procedures staff need to be aware of in relation to customer service (for example, after-service care)
   - the performance of the staff in relation to customer service
   - how you intend to monitor or are monitoring the customer service performance of your team
   - the importance of customer service.
2. distributing customer service policies and procedures to staff via email, notice-boards, memos and meetings
3. emails reminding staff of customer service standards
4. induction documentation which lists the customer service policies and procedures you have gone through with a new staff member

BTEC Unit 3: 1.1, 1.2, 2.1, 2.2, 2.3
NVQ Unit 40: 1.1, 1.2, 1.3

PUTTING IT INTO PRACTICE

This activity will enable your assessor to examine your competence by observing you carrying out workplace activities. This might include asking related questions to test your underpinning knowledge.

Conducting an induction interview

During this meeting, the assessor will be observing you:

1. outlining the customer service policies and procedures including:
   - customer complaints
   - customer queries
   - after sales
2. explaining the importance of customer service
3. explaining how the customer service performance is measured.

BTEC Unit 3: 1.1, 1.2, 2.1, 2.2, 2.3
NVQ Unit 40: 1.1, 1.2, 1.3, 2.1, 2.3

PROFESSIONAL DISCUSSION

Your assessor will conduct a professional discussion with you, which will capture evidence necessary to prove your level of knowledge and understanding of topic areas.

Below are some topic areas you will need to consider when preparing for the professional discussion with your assessor:

- the importance of customer service
- the importance of ensuring that your area of responsibility is up to date with customer service policies and procedures
- legislation that affects customer service
- the customer experience and how you manage it.

Your assessor will plan the content of your professional discussion and will advise you in order to help you to prepare beforehand. The professional discussion may cover more than this section of your Workbook.

Discussion process

The questioning process will offer you the opportunity to show how important customer service is within your organisation. It will also give you the opportunity to demonstrate your knowledge and understanding of customer service policies and procedures and the legislation that affects customer service.

To prepare for your professional discussion, you should think about how you could answer questions such as the following:

- Why is customer service important within your organisation?
- Why is it important to identify who your customers are?
- What customer service policies do you currently have in place?
- What needs and wants do your customers have?
- How do you communicate the customer service policies/procedures to your customers?
- What legislation must you be aware of that affects customer service?
- How does the Sale of Goods Act 1979 affect your organisation?

2. SUPPORTING YOUR TEAM IN MEETING CUSTOMER SERVICE STANDARDS

KNOWLEDGE AND UNDERSTANDING

Providing customer service and building positive working relationships with returning customers requires commitment from everyone in the organisation including your own team members.

Everyone should 'own the problem' when it comes to ensuring customers' satisfaction and this means that no one should assume they are immune to working towards and meeting customers' expectations.

To support your team, it is important that you communicate your customer service standards effectively so that they are clear about what is expected from them in different situations.

You will need to consider the ways in which you require your team members to:

- greet your customers (for example, eye-contact and a smile)
- deal with urgent and less urgent queries
- deal with complaints
- prioritise their actions to put the customer first
- work towards your organisation's accepted level of quality
- work flexibly to meet the needs of your customers
- keep your customers fully informed of delivery times and any delays
- work with colleagues (your internal customers) in other departments to meet your external customers' needs.

As a manager it is important that you lead by example, as your own behaviour towards your internal and external customers is bound to be noticed by your team members and others in the organisation.

Support can be offered to your team through:

- organising training sessions (for example, how to deal with complaints)
- agreeing departmental standards (for example, phones must be answered within six rings)
- producing and developing a customer service manual for all to use
- including 'customer service' as an agenda item in your team meetings

- sharing feedback from customers with your team
- thanking your team members when customers have been dealt with efficiently and effectively.

BTEC Unit 3: 1.2

Task 1

In the space below, write in your own descriptions of the following:

1. Managing the delivery of customer service within your team.

2. The ways in which you can offer support to your team to help them to meet your organisation's customer service standards.

Meeting the needs and expectations of different types of customer

Through your work as a manager, you are likely to work alongside different categories of customers at different times, as are your team members.

Apart from internal and external customers, you may liaise with customers who work at different stages in the supply chain, or within the channels of distribution. For example, you may supply raw materials to a manufacturer, which would make the manufacturer your customer.

BTEC Unit 3: 2.1

Task 2

Use the following table to consider the different categories of customers and then provide an example of each that relates to your own organisation. (An example has been done for you.)

4

Categories of customer	Example relating to your own organisation
Internal	*Colleagues in a different department*
External	
Wholesalers	
Retailers	
Service sector (for example. banks, insurance companies)	
Public sector organisations	
Manufacturers and producers	
Patients	
Clients	
Prospective customers	
Loyal customers	

Remember: You may have customers with particular needs. You and your team members should discuss how you will respond to customers with mobility, visual or hearing difficulties, or to customers of different ages or cultures, or who speak different languages.

The needs of your customers will vary depending on the nature of the business you are in and where you are in the supply chain.

Your customers' needs and expectations are likely to include:

- a speedy response to queries and requests for quotes
- delivery schedules to be adhered to and promises to be kept
- a quality product or service and value for money
- accurate information to be given when requested
- clear explanations of invoicing and credit/payment terms
- complaints to be dealt with speedily and effectively
- a telephone/email helpline
- an effective after-sales service
- warranties and guarantees
- friendly and helpful staff (throughout the organisation)
- to be listened to and taken seriously
- competitive prices.

You need to be aware of who your competitors are and how they deal with customer service. Speak to other managers in your organisation to find out if a 'competitor analysis' has been undertaken to compare your standards with theirs.

It is often a good idea to develop a unique selling point (USP) so that you stand apart from your competitors. This could be something such as free delivery which your competitors don't offer. Always discuss such strategies and ideas with your line manager and seek approval to make sure you are not working beyond your limits of authority.

BTEC Unit 3: 2.1

Task 3

Produce a bullet list of what you consider your own customer's needs and expectations to be. Write a short statement (approximately 250 words) to describe ways that you can meet these needs and expectations.

EVIDENCE GATHERING

In this activity you will identify an area of your work that will capture evidence of how you operate as a team leader. Your assessor will help you to identify suitable items of evidence.

BTEC Unit 3: 2.1
NVQ Unit 40: 2.1, 2.2, 2.3, 3.1, 3.2, 3.3, 3.4
WorkSkills Unit 5: 2.1

Offering support to staff about customer service issues

You need to gather evidence of activity within areas of your work to show your ability to do this. Suggested evidence may include:

1. staff rotas outlining the staff roles and responsibilities in relation to customer service
2. examples of emails where you are supporting and offering guidance to staff on how to deal with customer service issues
3. documents recommending/recording customer service training
4. minutes of meetings showing:
    - how you share out customer service roles and responsibilities in your area of responsibility
    - communication of feedback outcomes from staff/customers
    - communicating recommendations needed for improvements
5. action plans and/or development plans showing the customer service training needed.

Staff rotas not only outline roles and responsibilities, they also help employees to plan their working day effectively, helping them to ensure they are delivering the best possible service to customers.

BTEC Unit 3: 3.3
NVQ Unit 40: 2.1, 2.2, 3.3, 3.4

PUTTING IT INTO PRACTICE

Team meetings

This activity will enable your assessor to test your competence by observing you carrying out workplace activities. This might include related questions to test your underpinning knowledge.

The assessor will observe you in a team meeting:

- communicating the staff's roles and responsibilities in relation to customer service, such as who is in the complaints department, who will attend customer service training, etc.
- providing support and guidance in dealing with customer service issues and queries such as customer complaints
- reminding staff of the procedures for customer service
- discussing how to manage customer service.

PLTS EP: 1, 2, 3, 4

PLTS

This task will give you the chance to show your competency in the Effective Participators skill. Your assessor will assess your ability to discuss issues of concern with the team members, seek resolution wherever possible, present a persuasive case for action, suggest ways forward and try and influence others.

NVQ Unit 40: 2.1, 2.2, 2.3

PROFESSIONAL DISCUSSION

Your assessor will conduct a professional discussion with you, which will capture evidence necessary to prove your level of knowledge and understanding of topic areas.

Below are some topic areas you will need to consider when preparing for the professional discussion with your assessor:

- the techniques you use to support your staff when managing customer service
- the resources needed to meet customer service standards
- how to resolve customer service queries
- the organisational policies and procedures in relation to customer service.

Your assessor will plan the content of your professional discussion and will advise you in order to help you to prepare beforehand. The professional discussion may cover more than this section of your Workbook.

Discussion process

The questioning process will offer you the opportunity to show your understanding of how to manage a customer service problem following the organisational policies and procedures.

To prepare for your professional discussion, you should think about how you could answer questions such as the following:

- What resources do you need to meet customer service standards?
- Which organisational policies outline how to deal with customer service queries?
- Do you find coaching an effective way of supporting your staff?
- What customer service queries have you come across before? And how have you managed each query?
- Do you find a one-to-one discussion is more effective than a group discussion when managing customer service? Give reasons for your answer.

4

3. MONITORING AND EVALUATING CUSTOMER SERVICE PERFORMANCE, SYSTEMS AND PROCESSES

KNOWLEDGE AND UNDERSTANDING

Without the monitoring and evaluation of your customer service performance, it will be difficult to assess how effective your systems and procedures are and how satisfied your customers are.

As a manager, you should always be looking for ways to improve your customers' experience and this may require an examination of the processes you currently have in place with a view to making changes if required.

BTEC Unit 3: 2.3

Task 1

You will need to compare ways of improving your customers' experience. To help you to do this, you can use a decision list, as shown below. Complete the following table, based on your own current customer base. You should opt for the strategies that receive the most ticks.

Decision list (✓ = Yes / x = No)				
	Is it cost-effective?	**Will it affect profit positively?**	**Is this better than our major competitor?**	**Will it retain loyal customers?**
Decrease prices for customers				
Offer free delivery				
Respond to new enquiries in one day				

Of course, you can change the headings/questions in the table, to suit the nature of your business and the type of customer base you have.

When monitoring and evaluating your customers' satisfaction you will need to think about:

- how you will measure levels of satisfaction
- how much it will cost to measure levels of satisfaction
- the steps you will need to take to make changes in response to customer feedback and who you will need to seek approval from.

There are several ways in which you can monitor your customers' satisfaction. Some of these are:

- using mystery shoppers
- placing suggestion boxes in public areas
- asking staff for feedback
- obtaining verbal feedback from customers
- leaving 'comments cards' in public areas
- issuing questionnaires
- telephone surveys.

Remember: Monitoring customer satisfaction enables you to act upon problems and concerns before they escalate. You should consider that the strategy you use for monitoring purposes will affect the costs involved, the response rates and the time needed for the monitoring method.

BTEC Unit 3: 3.1

Task 2

You need to compare ways of monitoring customer service. In doing this you will need to think about the cost implications, response rates and the length of time the monitoring will take. Of course, the benefits must also be considered: if customer service is improved because of changes made in response to feedback, the benefits may outweigh the costs.

Consider the different ways you can conduct monitoring activity and write a brief account that compares and analyses the usefulness and effectiveness of each.

4

PLTS SM: 3, 4
EP: 2, 3

PLTS

This task will give you the opportunity to demonstrate your competence in Self-Manager and Effective Participator skills. You will need to take into consideration the risks of each technique and present a persuasive case for action.

Evaluating the customer service that you, your team members and others in the organisation provide is necessary, so that you understand how effective your systems and procedures are.

Through your evaluation process, you should be able to establish:

- who your repeat customers are
- the average spend per customer
- if there is a decrease/increase in customer complaints
- the number of new customers you have taken on
- the positive/negative feedback you have received and actions taken to respond to these factors
- how 'good press' (for example, articles and reports in trade magazines and newspapers) has increased your number of customers.

BTEC Unit 3: 3.2, 3.3

Task 3

Talk to other managers in your organisation and your own line manager to find out how your organisation currently evaluates its level of customer service and satisfaction. Based upon your findings, analyse the effectiveness of these techniques and describe the importance of making improvements to your organisation's customer service processes.

Monitoring and evaluating customer satisfaction is important to make sure your organisation:

- stays in business
- gains and retains customers
- gains loyal customers/clients
- maintains a good image and reputation
- promotes a caring and positive image
- performs better than your competitors.

4

BTEC Unit 3: 3.3

Task 4

Your organisation should concentrate on five major performance objectives so that it can work towards a concept of continuous improvement in relation to customer service. The five performance objectives are:

1. cost

2. quality

3. speed

4. dependability

5. flexibility.

Complete the different ways that your organisation can improve your customers experience, taking into consideration the five performance objectives below.

Performance objective	How your own organisation uses this objective to improve the customer experience	How your competitor uses this objective to improve the customer experience
Cost		
Quality		
Speed		
Dependability		
Flexibility		

WorkSkills Unit 5: 1.1, 1.2, 1.3, 1.4

Task 5a

It is important for you to understand the reasons why your customers rate your work highly or find it necessary to complain.

PLTS IE: 1, 2, 3, 4, 5
EP: 2
SM: 2, 3, 4
CT: 1, 2, 3

PLTS

…is task will give you the opportunity to demonstrate your Independent Enquirers, Effective Participators, …elf-Managers and Creative Thinkers skills. This task requires you to carry out research and to prepare a …tionnaire based on your research. The second part of … task requires you to analyse the responses received to the questionnaire sent out.

You need to have a plan of action for carrying out some research that will enable you to make changes to the way you and your team work, in the light of any problems that customers highlight. (Remember: some of the changes you need to make may need approval from your line manager.)

1. Generate some questions that you can incorporate into a customer feedback questionnaire that is related to specific problems such as speed of delivery or quality of goods and services provided.

2. Produce a questionnaire that incorporates the questions you have identified and send this out to your internal and external customers. (Obtain permission from your line manager before doing this.)

A copy of your questionnaire will be used as evidence in your portfolio.

WorkSkills Unit 5: 2.1, 2.2, 2.3, 2.4

Task 5b

Your questionnaire response rate will vary depending on the nature of your business and the relationships you have with your customers.

1. Evaluate the usefulness and relevance of the responses you have received.

2. What factors (for example, time constraints) influenced your research process?

3. Assess whether you used the right type of questions to get the responses you expected.

4. Analyse whether your findings meet the research questions.

5. Assess any assumptions made within your research methodology (for example, the customers you targeted).

4

WorkSkills Unit 5: 2.5

Task 5c

What would have been the impact of using alternative research methods to obtain your data?

EVIDENCE GATHERING

In this activity you will identify an area of your work that will capture evidence of how you operate as a team leader. Your assessor will help you to identify suitable items of evidence.

NVQ Unit 40: 3.1, 3.2, 3.3, 3.4
WorkSkills Unit 5: 1.1, 1.2, 1.3, 1.4, 2.1, 2.2, 2.3, 2.4, 2.5

An evaluation of the customer service performance within your area of responsibility

You need to gather evidence of activity within areas of your work to demonstrate your ability to do this. Suggested evidence may include:

1. prepared feedback sheets
2. action plans showing how you will carry out the research
3. emails from managers requesting this research to take place
4. emails to managers outlining the proposal of the research
5. feedback sheets prepared and given to staff and customers
6. customer service performance criteria (for example, Key Performance Indicators (KPIs), percentage of returns)

Evaluating the service you provide for your customers can help you to identify changes that will improve what you do.

7. report on feedback outcomes from staff/customers to include:

- evaluation of the feedback
- identifying areas for improvements
- recommendations for changes.

NVQ Unit 40: 3.1, 3.2, 3.3

PUTTING IT INTO PRACTICE

This activity will enable your assessor to test your competence by observing you carrying out workplace activities. This might include related questions to test your underpinning knowledge.

The assessor will observe you in a team meeting:

- providing feedback on the results of a recent survey
- providing feedback on the results of customer service performance criteria (for example, KPIs, complaint numbers)
- discussing why performance criteria have not been achieved
- providing feedback and recognition when performance criteria have been achieved
- encouraging the team to suggest areas for improvement
- recommending areas for change.

BTEC Unit 3: 3.2, 3.3
NVQ Unit 40: 3.1, 3.2, 3.3, 3.4
WorkSkills Unit 5: 1.1, 1.2, 1.3, 1.4, 2.1, 2.2, 2.3, 2.4, 2.5

PROFESSIONAL DISCUSSION

Your assessor will conduct a professional discussion with you, which will capture evidence necessary to prove your level of knowledge and understanding of topic areas.

Below are some topic areas you will need to consider when preparing for the professional discussion with your assessor:

- criteria used to monitor customer service performance (i.e. KPIs)
- techniques used to evaluate and monitor customer service performance
- how to analyse feedback from staff and customers
- how you make informed and effective recommendations to improve customer service
- the importance of encouraging the team to think creatively
- the importance of obtaining the team's views on why the criteria have not been met.

Your assessor will plan the content of your professional discussion and will advise you in order to help you to prepare beforehand. The professional discussion may cover more than this section of your Workbook.

Discussion process

The questioning process will offer you the opportunity to show how to monitor customer service within your area of responsibility.

To prepare for your professional discussion, you should think about how you could answer questions such as the following:

- What techniques do you currently use to monitor customer satisfaction?
- Why is it important to make improvements to customer service?
- How do you make informed decisions on customer service standards?
- What assumptions did you make when carrying out the research on customer service?
- How did you manage these assumptions?
- What other research methods could you have used?
- Why didn't you use the other research methods?

5

The success of an organisation depends upon each manager's ability to foster positive working relationships in their teams. This ensures everyone is able to concentrate on achieving their individual, departmental and organisational objectives.

In this section you will find a range of activities to help you prepare and gather evidence for your assessment in relation to the following topics:

1. Developing working relationships with team members
2. Maintaining working relationships with team members

It has already been established that the ability of your organisation to achieve its business objectives depends upon teams and departments within the organisation meeting their own targets.

This means that developing effective and productive working relationships within your team is one of your key responsibilities. It is important that you understand your part in leading your team. As manager, it is your responsibility to make sure that tasks are completed on time and that any difficulties are not allowed to escalate into situations that affect the morale and motivation of the whole team.

This section will offer you the opportunity to evaluate your knowledge and understanding of the characteristics of productive working relationships between you and your team, and between your team members.

5

1. DEVELOPING WORKING RELATIONSHIPS WITH TEAM MEMBERS

KNOWLEDGE AND UNDERSTANDING

It is important that the skills, attributes and expertise of your team members are put to good use. A team within which everyone expects to carry out the same task on a daily basis is going to be unproductive. This means that you need to coordinate activities to take account of each team member's skills and attributes.

When planning and allocating tasks, it will be beneficial for you to know and understand the preferred role of each team member, what they feel they are good at and what they feel they can achieve.

Features of productive working relationships include:

- careful allocation of responsibilities
- clear lines of communication
- treating everyone fairly and equally
- involving team members in decision making
- sharing feedback on performance
- prioritising tasks
- keeping promises
- being approachable
- being polite and courteous
- conflict management
- identifying strengths and weaknesses of team members
- giving praise as appropriate.

Sharing feedback on performance in a polite and courteous way can help to develop positive working relationships with team members.

BTEC Unit 9: 1.1

Task 1a

Reflect on the bullet list opposite and identify features of productive working relationships that exist within your own team. Then list and describe what these are in the space below.

Once you have identified the features of productive working relationships, you may find it useful to think about the benefits attached to them. Some of these benefits will be:

- shared vision and commitment to achieving team objectives
- sharing ideas and concerns
- enhanced individual performance
- improved customer satisfaction and reduction in complaints
- work being completed in a timely fashion
- improved communication between team members
- increased levels of morale and motivation
- increased quality of output and less wastage
- a willingness to assist each other when behind schedule.

In the late 1970s, management theorist Meredith Belbin created a questionnaire that identified roles or categories that team members may fall into. Belbin's view is that for a team to work effectively, it is necessary for it to be made up of members who have qualities and attributes that complement each other. Belbin suggests that a team that has a mix of specific roles contained within it will outperform a team that does not contain such a mix. (You could invite your team members to complete Belbin's questionnaire to identify their own roles. Go to www.belbin.com for more information.)

BTEC Unit 9: 1.2

Task 1b

It is important for you to identify the benefits of productive working relationships. Belbin's nine roles each describe characteristics and attributes that your team members may possess. Now respond to the two activities below:

1. Research into Belbin's nine roles and write an account of which role type best describes the personality and characteristics of each of your team members.

2. Add a paragraph to your account above that outlines the benefit to you of knowing your team members' identified roles.

BTEC Unit 9: 2.1

Task 2

Another theorist, by the name of Tuckman, studied the development of teams and concluded that a group of people in a given situation work through a series of stages before they become an effective team. Tuckman's stages are listed in the following table. Spend some time researching into each of them and then complete the table by writing in your description of each stage and, alongside it, a real-life example where you can apply each stage (perhaps based on the team you manage now).

Description of each stage of development	**Real-life example in your workplace**
Forming *When a team first comes together, there can be power struggles and/or conflict as people are unsure of each other*	
Storming	
Norming	
Performing	
Mourning	

Behaving professionally when working with team members

Leading by example can influence the behaviour of your team members. Your own behaviours will be observed by your team and it is important for you to nurture and develop a culture of professionalism. Observations of your behaviour will include:

- your management style and how you delegate work
- your approach to fairness and equality
- your ability to listen and respond to the views of others
- your approachability and willingness to support others
- your ability to recognise your own limitations
- your ability to deal with negativity and difficulties appropriately and swiftly
- your ability to communicate effectively both verbally and non-verbally
- your approach to managing performance and quality assurance.

5

It is worthwhile assessing your own behaviour and benchmarking this against how others may see you. For example, you may think you are assertive in your approach, whereas your team members may think that you are aggressive. Asking for honest feedback from others may, if required, prompt you to alter your behaviour and instil harmony in your workplace.

BTEC Unit 9: 2.1

Task 3

How would you describe the professional behaviour a manager should possess when working with team members?

Communicating successfully with team members

Communication can be described as 'getting the right message to the right people at the right time', and then obtaining feedback.

If you were to bake a cake you would need to include the right ingredients for your cake to rise successfully in the oven. Similarly, if you want your business organisation to rise successfully, ahead of its competitors, then the ingredients have to be right. One of the most important ingredients is that of communication.

Effective communication of knowledge and information to your team members can help you to:

- build positive working relationships
- get to know your team members better
- provide records of discussions and actions undertaken
- keep everyone informed
- gain trust and respect.

Team meetings, briefings, one-to-one supervisions, emails and reports are some of the ways in which a manager can communicate knowledge and information to team members.

You should think carefully about how effective two-way communication with your team members can help to raise levels of morale and motivation, leading to improved performance, output and customer satisfaction.

BTEC Unit 9: 2.2

Task 4

1. Research into the work of Wilbur Schramm, who designed and produced a communication model. Find out what he meant by:

a. Encoder

b. Decoder

2. Describe ways in which a manager can successfully communicate knowledge and information to team members.

When communicating you can use:

- **formal methods** – scheduled and minuted meetings with agendas, formal reports, staff appraisals, disciplinary and grievance hearings, committee meetings
- **informal methods** – one-to-one supervisions, informal memos and reports, briefings and de-briefings, emails, telephone calls, task and finish group meetings, quality circles.

Different circumstances will dictate the techniques you will use to help you to communicate effectively with colleagues.

A task and finish group is made up of employees from different departments within an organisation, with appropriate skills and experience, who are selected to oversee a project over a period of time, such as reviewing fire procedures.

Also, when communicating you need to think about the techniques you will use. These are likely to vary depending upon the circumstances you find yourself in, but may include:

- letters
- emails
- reports
- meetings
- telephone calls
- video-conferencing
- surveys
- appraisals
- texts (for business purposes)
- social networking (for business purposes).

BTEC Unit 9: 2.3, 2.4

Task 5

Communicating effectively with your team members can help you to develop positive working relationships with them.

1. Identify and select the most appropriate methods you feel you should use when communicating with your team.

2. Look back at the methods you selected above and, in the space below, give reasons why you selected each one.

EVIDENCE GATHERING

In this activity you will identify an area of your work that will capture evidence of how you operate as a team leader. Your assessor will help you to identify suitable items of evidence.

NVQ Unit 15: 2.1, 2.2, 4.1

Establishing a working relationship with colleagues

You need to gather evidence of activity within areas of your work to demonstrate your ability to do this. Suggested evidence may include:

1. emails to colleagues outlining their roles and responsibilities in relation to a specific task
2. minutes of meetings detailing the information that was given to colleagues
3. project proposals including:
    - action plans showing colleagues' roles and responsibilities
    - allocation of tasks to individuals
    - staff rotas outlining roles and responsibilities
    - emails to managers agreeing the roles and responsibilities of your colleagues.

BTEC Unit 9: 2.1, 2.3, 2.4
NVQ Unit 15: 2.1, 2.2, 3.1, 4.1

PUTTING IT INTO PRACTICE

This activity will enable your assessor to examine your competence by observing you carrying out workplace activities. This might include asking related questions to test your underpinning knowledge.

a. Observation of a project and/or team meeting

Your assessor will be assessing you carrying out the following:

- interacting with the team
- identifying and communicating with colleagues from your own department and those from other organisations
- discussing and agreeing the roles and responsibilities of your colleagues
- encouraging your colleagues to participate in the discussions
- building a rapport with your colleagues
- clarifying your understanding of information given by other team members
- presenting information in way that is clear and concise.

b. Formal or informal discussions with colleagues

Your assessor will be assessing you on the following:

- the techniques you use to communicate important information
- using various methods to communicate to your colleagues
- rephrasing questions and reiterating information to make sure you are clear
- emphasising important points, perhaps through the use of appropriate body language
- how professional you are when communicating with your colleagues
- managing a conflict situation.

BTEC Unit 1: 2.2
Unit 9: 1.1, 1.2, 2.1, 2.2
NVQ Unit 15: 1.1, 2.1, 2.2, 3.1, 4.1, 4.2

PROFESSIONAL DISCUSSION

Your assessor will conduct a professional discussion with you, which will capture evidence necessary to prove your level of knowledge and understanding of topic areas.

Below are some topic areas you will need to consider when preparing for the professional discussion with your assessor:

- features and benefits of productive working relationships
- who your colleagues are internally and externally to your organisation
- how you build a productive working relationship with internal and external colleagues
- factors you need to take into consideration when discussing and agreeing roles and responsibilities for colleagues
- being professional
- techniques used to share information with others
- managing conflict situations.

Your assessor will plan the content of your professional discussion and will advise you in order to help you to prepare beforehand. The professional discussion may cover more than this section of your Workbook.

Discussion process

The questioning process will offer you the opportunity to demonstrate your understanding of the importance of having a good working relationship with your team, the effects of having a poor working relationship with your team, and how you manage conflict situations.

To prepare for your professional discussion, you should think about how you could answer questions such as the following:

- What can cause a non-productive working relationship?
- How do you build a good working relationship with your team and your colleagues?
- Why is it important to have a good working relationship with your colleagues?
- How do you make sure you are professional when interacting with internal and external colleagues?
- Why is it important to clarify your understanding of information given by others?
- How do you communicate with your colleagues?
- How do you / would you manage individual conflict?
- How do you / would you manage group conflict differently from managing conflict between two members?

2. MAINTAINING WORKING RELATIONSHIPS WITH TEAM MEMBERS

KNOWLEDGE AND UNDERSTANDING

Your work as a manager will require you to build positive working relationships with your team members if you are to minimise the risk of conflict and difficulties, and work holistically to meet targets.

Maintaining a rapport and creating a culture of harmony will help you and your team to adopt a collaborative approach to meeting targets.

Adopting a positive approach when working with team members

Very often, positive thinking and a positive approach to work tasks and problem solving can result in a team performing well and as a result having increased output.

Employing a consultative style of working will encourage your team members to share ideas and views with you and with each other. This can serve to enhance the quality of work being carried out, reduce costs, speed up processes and satisfy your customer's needs.

If you have a positive approach, you may:

- resolve problems and difficulties with greater speed
- lessen the risk of disagreements within the team
- be more decisive
- praise team members more regularly
- encourage suggestions, views and ideas from others.

Encouraging your team members to share their ideas and views can speed up processes and create a culture of harmony.

5

BTEC Unit 9: 3.1

Task 1

Examine the working relationships between you and your team members.

1. In the space below, describe the importance of adopting a positive approach when dealing with your team members.

2. Conduct some research into the work of management theorist Kurt Lewin. As a supporter of three main leadership and management styles (Autocratic, Democratic and Laissez-faire), his view was that there may be times when managers need to use each style, but the democratic style is most likely to encourage employee involvement in decision making.

Once you have carried out your research, complete the table below:

Lewin's management style	**Circumstances in which it is most likely to be used**	**To what degree it will assist a manager to adopt a positive approach with team workers**
Autocratic		
Democratic		
Laissez-faire		

Remember: Your objectives and targets need to be SMART and it is important to be open, honest and transparent about times when it would appear that targets are not likely to be met. If you communicate this and address the actions that are needed, your team members are likely to respect you more than if you simply chastise them at a later date for not meeting targets!

Resolving work-related difficulties that arise with teams

Difficulties in the workplace, if left unchallenged, can lead to:

- lowered morale and motivation
- a blame culture
- conflict situations and bullying
- aggressive behaviour
- lowered productivity and output
- reduced levels of performance
- increased risks of accidents
- lowered quality, re-working of products and increased waste
- unhappy customers
- disciplinary issues and grievances
- unethical and discriminatory behaviours.

It is important for you to step in at the earliest opportunity to prevent the situation from escalating and getting out of control.

When managing difficult behaviour, you should consider:

- discussing the situation with those concerned as early as possible
- negotiating a fair outcome and a compromise to suit all parties
- examining alternative courses of action
- being tough on the problem, not the people involved
- staying calm and assertive at all times
- referring those involved to appropriate policies and procedures
- being aware of your own capabilities and limits of authority (you may need to seek advice from your line manager or others in the organisation).

It should be made clear to your team members that unacceptable behaviour will not be tolerated, and will be challenged by you and other managers. This message can be communicated with tact and diplomacy, through team meetings, workplace policies, newsletters or your organisation's code of conduct.

5

BTEC Unit 9: 3.2
NVQ Unit 15: 5.2

Task 2

Dealing with work-related difficulties is never easy. Those directly involved and those who are not will look to you to find some type of resolution. The longer a situation persists, the more damaging it can be to your team and the team's work.

1. Explain how you would resolve identified potential difficulties.

2. Complete the table below to compare ways of resolving work-related difficulties that arise in teams.

Ways to resolve difficulties	Advantages	Disadvantages
Negotiating a fair outcome and/or compromise	*Can restore harmony, resume normal working and build team spirit*	*Manager may be perceived as weak and one party may feel that they have been disadvantaged and unfairly treated*
Being tough on the problem, not the people		
Staying calm and assertive at all times		
Referring those involved to appropriate policies and procedures		
Examining alternative courses of action		

Leading by example and taking time to support your team members can help to develop relationships.

During your career as a manager, you may at some point find that you have some team members who require more support than others. These people may fall into the category of 'can't do' people or 'won't do' people. 'Can't do' team members are easier to deal with, as they are willing to improve and work hard, but perhaps need further training and support. Your 'won't do' team members are unlikely to improve, regardless of how much support you offer and it may, unfortunately, eventually lead to the instigation of disciplinary procedures.

Remember: Your team members will be observing your own behaviour, and by leading by example you can contribute to the development of positive working relationships.

In order to complete tasks on time, it will be necessary to delegate work to your team. There are a number of factors that need to be taken into consideration when delegating work such as their skills and knowledge and their workload.

BTEC Unit 1: 3.1

Task 3a

Describe the importance and purpose of delegation.

5

BTEC Unit 1: 3.2

Task 3b

Using workplace examples, describe ways of coordinating delegated work.

BTEC Unit 1: 3.3

Task 3c

There are many barriers to delegation. Complete the table below using workplace examples wherever possible.

Psychological barrier	How you managed/would manage the situation
Your fear of losing control	
Your lack of confidence	
Your lack of knowledge and/or skills to complete the task	
Team members' fear of criticism	
Team members' resistance to change	
Lack of rewards	
Team members' fear of failure	

EVIDENCE GATHERING

In this activity you will identify an area of your work that will capture evidence of how you operate as a team leader. Your assessor will help you to identify suitable items of evidence.

You need to gather evidence of activity within areas of your work to demonstrate your ability to do the folllowing:

NVQ Unit 3: 1.1, 1.2, 2.1, 2.2, 2.3, 3.1

a. Planning, allocating work and adopting a positive approach with your team

Suggested evidence may include:

1. minutes of meetings, including:
    - a discussion about team objectives between you and your manager
    - discussions with the team about the plans that have been set
    - how you outlined the standards of work expected
    - a record of how the work has been allocated
2. staff rotas
3. action plans outlining the team's objectives and how they will achieve these objectives
4. emails in which you discuss the team objectives with your manager
5. emails to the team outlining the team objectives
6. a skill scan completed on the team
7. development or training plans of a team member identifying the need to increase skills to meet the team objectives
8. planning tools (for example, Gantt charts, work planner, diaries) which outline the team's SMART objectives
9. emails where you have provided answers and guidance to your team.

NVQ Unit 3: 4.1, 4.3, 5.1, 5.2, 5.3
Unit 15: 5.1

b. Team member performance

Suggested evidence may include:

1. Personal Development Review documentation:
    - assessing team members' work against standards, for example Key Performance Indicators (KPIs)
    - discussing conflict situations and how to manage them
    - recording why the team member is not meeting their objectives
    - reviewing their performance
    - giving positive feedback and suggestions on areas for improvement (for example, attending time management training)
2. minutes of meetings:
    - reviewing progress to the team
    - providing feedback on targets met or not met

5

Open discussions can help to implement new ideas to improve the performance of your team members.

PLTS IE: 1, 2, 3, 4, 5, 6

PLTS

By completing this task you will have the opportunity to demonstrate your competence in Independent Enquirer skills. This task will allow you to demonstrate your ability to ask relevant questions to resolve a problem, explore reasons for a problem, judge the relevance of information and make an informed decision.

- identifying reasons for not achieving the objectives
- brainstorms or discussions on how to improve team performance, perhaps through additional resources or time, or new skills
- implementing new ideas to improve team performance, such as changes to team structure, change of team leader, obtaining new resources

3. control boards – monitoring KPIs and team objectives.

BTEC Unit 1: 2.2
NVQ Unit 3: 4.2
Unit 15: 5.1

c. Monitoring conflict situations

Suggested evidence may include:

1. emailing the bullying and harassment policy to all team members

2. reminding staff via email about the grievance and disciplinary procedures

3. offering counselling to team members

4. reminding staff of the external agencies who are available to help with conflict.

BTEC Unit 1: 2.2
NVQ Unit 3: 2.1, 2.2, 2.3, 4.1, 4.2, 4.3, 5.1, 5.2, 5.3
Unit 15: 5.1

PUTTING IT INTO PRACTICE

This activity will enable your assessor to examine your competence by observing you carrying out workplace activities. This might include asking related questions to test your underpinning knowledge.

a. Observation of team meeting

During this observation, your assessor will be assessing you on the following:

- discussing with your team the work that needs to be done and to what standard
- agreeing SMART objectives with the team
- providing guidance and support on specific issues relating to the team's objectives
- delegating tasks to individuals based on their capabilities and capacity to take more work on
- communicating clearly so that all team members understand.

b. Control boards'/performance planning boards' team discussion

- assessing the team's performance against objectives
- identifying the reasons or causes for not meeting objectives
- identifying the tasks and objectives that have been completed and providing feedback.

c. Team meeting debriefings

PLTS TW: 1, 2, 3, 4, 5, 6

> **PLTS**
>
> As a result of this observation, you will be given the opportunity to demonstrate Team Worker skills. You will collaborate with others during the discussions, hopefully reach agreements, adapt your behaviour to deal with different situations, and provide constructive feedback and support.

- discussion on which targets have been achieved
- questioning to find out why objectives haven't been met
- identifying causes of not achieving the objectives
- finding out the reasons behind a conflict of interest in the team and suggesting solutions to reduce this
- discussing potential work-related difficulties and how to overcome these.

PROFESSIONAL DISCUSSION

BTEC Unit 1: 2.2, 3.1, 3.2, 3.3
NVQ Unit 3: 2.1, 2.2, 2.3, 3.1, 4.1, 4.2, 4.3, 5.1, 5.2, 5.3

Your assessor will conduct a professional discussion with you, which will capture evidence necessary to prove your level of knowledge and understanding of topic areas.

Below are some topic areas you will need to consider when preparing for the professional discussion with your assessor:

- the importance of discussing plans with your team
- the importance of delegating
- allocating work to team members
- setting SMART objectives with team members
- standards of work

5

One-to-one discussions can enable you to give constructive feedback to your team members when objectives have not been met.

- supporting your team in order to achieve team objectives
- reasons why the team members have not achieved their objectives
- compare the different ways you can manage situations of conflict between your team members
- tools used to monitor and evaluate performance of your team
- monitoring and dealing with conflict
- how to improve team performance
- giving constructive feedback to improve team performance.

Your assessor will plan the content of your professional discussion and will advise you in order to help you to prepare beforehand. The professional discussion may cover more than this section of your Workbook.

Discussion process

The questioning process will offer you the opportunity to show how you delegate work to your team and what factors need to be taken into consideration when this is done, and how to support an individual during times of struggle and underperformance. To prepare for your professional discussion, you should think about how you could answer questions such as the following:

- Can delegating work motivate your team?
- How do you make sure you delegate work to the right individual?
- Is it necessary sometimes to delegate work to a team member who has very little knowledge of the task? If so, why?
- Why is it important to agree and set SMART objectives with your team?
- How do you make sure all team members are aware of the standard of work expected?
- What organisational quality standards do you need to be aware of?
- How do you communicate these standards to your team?
- How do you manage 'problem people'?
- What tools do you use to monitor the performance of your team?
- Do you use one-to-one meetings or team briefs to identify why the team have not achieved their objectives? Give reasons for your answer.
- What techniques do you use to improve the performance of your team?
- How do you give feedback?
- Why is it important to give constructive feedback to your team?

Employment Rights and Responsibilities

As you work through this section, you will need to be clear about your own understanding of your occupation, the industry in which you work and the sector in which your organisation is located.

In this section, the range of activities that you undertake will help you prepare for assessment in relation to Employment Rights and Responsibilities:

cfa business skills @ work

1. statutory rights and responsibilities
2. procedures and documents within your organisation
3. sources of information and advice about employment rights and responsibilities
4. about your occupation and organisation
5. occupations and career pathways
6. representative bodies relevant to you and your organisation

HOW TO USE THIS SECTION

This ERR section of your BTEC Apprenticeship Assessment Workbook has been produced by the Council for Administration (CfA) to ensure that you know about your Employment Rights and Responsibilities (ERR), which form part of your Apprenticeship programme.

As you are currently undertaking one of the Apprenticeship programmes in business skills, you will have a business-related job role. Because there are many types of business across every sector of the UK economy, we know that apprentices completing this book will be working in a wide variety of settings, from education to construction.

In distinguishing between what we mean by job role, industry and sector when they are mentioned in this guide, the following table below will help you. It contains examples, but remember, this is not a complete list of job roles.

Job role	Industry	Sector
Team leader	Local authority	Public services

As you look through this ERR section you will note that there are two main areas under each of the section headings:

What you should know

You will find a list of ERR statements that you need to know as part of your induction programme.

Over to you

You will find a few questions designed to check that you know and understand certain aspects of ERR.

You do not need to complete the entire ERR section straight away, nor do you have to work through it in any particular order. You should talk to people such as your line manager, training provider or mentor (if you have one) for information, help and advice on some of the areas. You will also need to do some research using your staff manual and (if available) on the internet.

1. STATUTORY RIGHTS AND RESPONSIBILITIES

All candidates need to know that employers and employees have a range of statutory responsibilities and rights under employment law, and that employment can be affected by other legislation as well.

1.1 CONTRACTS OF EMPLOYMENT[1]

What you should know

How an employer and employee (you) are governed by the terms and conditions contained within a contract of employment (this may not be in writing).

- Employment contracts are legally binding on both the employer and employee and serve to protect each other's rights and responsibilities.
- The terms (legal parts) of the contract can be in a variety of forms, including:
  - verbal agreement
  - in a written contract (or similar document)
  - in an employee handbook or on a company notice board
  - in an offer letter from your employer
  - required by law (for example, your employer must pay you at least the minimum wage)
  - in collective agreements
  - implied terms.
- A contract of employment comes into force as soon as a firm offer of employment has been made and accepted, even if agreement has only been verbal, e.g. at an interview.
- By law, all employees are entitled to a written statement of the key terms and conditions of their employment within two months of starting work, providing the contract is to last for more than one month.
- Conditions of employment can relate to the employee (notice periods, salary/wages, benefits, work hours) or to the company (discipline/grievance procedures and other things required by law).
- Employment contracts may be open-ended (permanent); for temporary periods of employment or for fixed terms; or for full or part-time work.

1 Information from www.direct.gov.uk (Crown Copyright)

- Changes to employment contracts must be made following procedures, which are designed to protect the employee from unfair treatment and ensure consultation on the nature of any changes proposed.
- A code of practice exists in case of any conflicts between an individual employee and their employer. There is no legally binding process for this, but the organisation's grievance procedures should comply with the code.
- Employees who believe they have been dismissed or otherwise treated unfairly may be able to take their case to an independent Employment Tribunal.
- There are three types of employment status, which indicates a person's rights and responsibilities at work: 'worker', 'employee' or 'self-employed'.
    - 'Workers' include people working under a variety of contracts. Employees are workers, but have different rights and responsibilities than workers.
    - 'Employees' are workers, but employees have a wider range of employment rights and responsibilities than other workers (for example, the requirement to give notice if you wish to leave your job).
    - 'Self-employed' people are not generally covered by employment law, except for some things such as health and safety. Rights and responsibilities are determined by the person's contract with their client.
- Termination of an employment contract is governed by rules and rights, which protect the employee and employer from unfair treatment.

Businesses in the European Union (EU) that employ at least 20 employees must meet some minimum requirements for informing and consulting employees.

Under Directive 2002/14/EC, a business must keep its employees informed of:

- what the business is doing and the economic situation it faces
- what the employment situation is within the business
- any decisions likely to lead to substantial changes in the work organisation or contractual relations.

You must also make sure employees' representatives have the time and information to carry out an adequate study and, where necessary, prepare for consultation.

Over to you

You will need to know about your contract of employment and/or written terms and conditions statement, the systems and policies and procedures in place to protect your rights and responsibilities and those of your employer.

Task 1

What legislation exists to recognise and protect your terms and conditions of employment on the grounds of sex, marital status, race or disability?

The terms of an employment contract set out what you and your employer can expect of each other. There are several different types and some do not need to be written down in your employment contract. If there's anything in your contract that you're unsure about, or which is confusing, ask your employer to explain it to you.

WorkSkills Unit 2: 2.1

Task 2

You should know what is a legally binding part of your contract and what is not. The legal parts of a contract are known as 'terms'. Contract terms can come from a number of different sources.

Can you give at least three examples of legally binding contract terms?

1.	
2.	
3.	

Task 3

There are three types of employment status: a 'worker', an 'employee' or 'self-employed'.

Find out the basic employment rights for each employment status. Name at least three in each category.

Worker	Employee	Self-employed
1.	1.	1.
2.	2.	2.
3.	3.	3.

WorkSkills Unit 2: 2.3

Task 4

You also need to know what you should do if you have a grievance about the terms and conditions of your employment. This may be related to your working hours, for example.

If you had a grievance in the workplace, who would you go to?

Name:	
Job title:	

1.2 ANTI-DISCRIMINATION[2]

The Equality Act 2010 combines previous anti-discrimination legislation into one act, and covers race, sex, sexual orientation, disability, religion or belief, gender reassignment, pregnancy and maternity, marriage and civil partnership, and age. It protects against discrimination, harassment and victimisation.

The sex discrimination aspect of the law relates to all types of UK organisations, and covers:

- recruitment
- employment terms and conditions
- pay and benefits
- training
- promotion and transfer opportunities
- redundancy
- dismissal.

2 Information from www.direct.gov.uk (Crown Copyright)

Everyone has the right to receive equal pay for work of the same value, regardless of whether they are a man or woman.

All aspects of employment (or prospective employment) are protected from age discrimination, including:

- recruitment
- employment terms and conditions
- promotions and transfers
- training
- dismissals.

All training and promotion opportunities should be publicised to all employees and open to everyone on a fair and equal basis, regardless of age.

Employers cannot discriminate against workers because of a physical or mental disability, nor can they fail to make reasonable adjustments to accommodate a worker with a disability. The Equality Act 2010 covers the following in relation to disability:

- application forms
- interview arrangements
- aptitude or proficiency tests
- job offers
- terms of employment including pay
- promotion, transfer and training opportunities
- work-related benefits, such as access to recreation or refreshment facilities
- dismissal or redundancy
- discipline and grievances.

Anti-discrimination law also protects employees who have made a complaint or intend to complain about unfair treatment.

EU anti-discrimination law has been adopted across all member states, including the UK.

Just as in the UK, if you employ anyone within the EU, you must make sure that you do not discriminate against them because of their racial or ethnic origin, religion or belief, disability, age, or sexual orientation. This means:

- giving everyone in your company equal treatment at work and access to training
- making sure that disabled people can work comfortably
- providing equal access to employment
- having an equal pay system.

Over to you

You will need to know about the equal opportunities policies and procedures in your workplace and any exemptions from the law that are relevant to your occupation.

Sex discrimination

An employer cannot discriminate against you because:

- of your sex
- you are married or a civil partner
- you have gone through, are going through or intend to go through gender reassignment (this means someone who changes their sex under medical supervision).

Positive action

In some circumstances, the law allows an employer to encourage or offer support specifically to men or women (called 'positive action').

For example, an employer who has no female managers might offer some training in management skills only to women, or encourage them to apply for management jobs.

In some cases, a job can be offered to someone of a particular sex because of what is called a 'genuine occupational qualification'. Examples could include:

- some jobs in single-sex schools
- jobs in some welfare services
- acting jobs that need a man or a woman.[3]

Task 5

Give three examples of aspects that are covered by sex discrimination law.

1.	
2.	
3.	

3 Information from www.direct.gov.uk (Crown Copyright)

Task 6

Give three examples of when sex discrimination does not apply.

1.	
2.	
3.	

1.3 AGE DISCRIMINATION

Under the Equality Act 2010, you cannot be denied a job, equal chance of training or promotion based on your age, nor can you be harassed or victimised because of it.

The act applies to all employers, private and public sector, the voluntary sector, vocational training providers, trade unions, professional organisations and employer organisations. However, some work activities can only be undertaken by a person over a minimum age.

Employers can't discriminate on the basis of age during recruitment. Your skills should be considered, rather than your age. Job descriptions should not refer to age (either specifically or by using language that implies an age, such as 'mature' and 'young' or 'energetic') unless this can be justified. Experience, skills and ability should be considered when these are equivalent to qualifications.

According to the law, it is not permitted on the grounds of age to:

- discriminate directly against you – that is, to treat you less favourably than others because of your age – unless it can be objectively justified
- discriminate indirectly against you – that is, to apply a practice which would disadvantage you because of your age – unless it can be objectively justified
- subject you to harassment – that is, unwanted conduct that violates your dignity or creates an intimidating, hostile, degrading, humiliating or offensive environment
- victimise you because you have made or intend to make a complaint or allegation or have given or intend to give evidence in relation to a complaint of discrimination on grounds of age
- discriminate against you, in certain circumstances, after the working relationship has ended.[4]

4 Information from www.direct.gov.uk (Crown Copyright)

Task 7

Name five aspects of employment relating to age that fall under the protection of the Equality Act 2010.

1.	
2.	
3.	
4.	
5.	

Task 8

Name three examples of age discrimination that could occur during the recruitment process.

1.	
2.	
3.	

1.4 DISABILITY DISCRIMINATION[5]

The Equality Act 2010 makes it unlawful to:

- discriminate directly against you – that is, to treat you less favourably than others because of your disability, or because of something connected with your disability, or because you are associated with (e.g. care for) someone with a disability
- discriminate indirectly against you – that is, to apply a practice which would disadvantage you because of your disability unless it can be objectively justified
- subject you to harassment – that is, unwanted conduct that violates your dignity or creates an intimidating, hostile, degrading, humiliating or offensive environment
- victimise you because you have made or intend to make a complaint or allegation, or have given or intend to give evidence in relation to a complaint of discrimination on grounds of disability
- ask questions, except in certain circumstances, about your health before offering you a job.

5 Information from www.direct.gov.uk (Crown Copyright)

Task 9

Give three examples of disability discrimination.

1.	
2.	
3.	

1.5 WORKING HOURS, REST BREAKS AND HOLIDAY ENTITLEMENTS[6]

What you should know

There are working time regulations (Working Time Directive and Working Time Regulations 1998) that apply to all employers in the UK, regardless of sector or organisation size.

The weekly maximum working hours for adult workers cannot be more than 48 hours per week, on average. Your working week is not covered by the working time limits if you have signed a voluntary opt-out agreement (you can only do this if you are 18 or over), or if you have a job:

- where you can choose freely how long you will work (e.g. a managing executive)
- in the armed forces, emergency services and police – in some circumstances
- as a domestic servant in private houses
- as a sea transport worker, a mobile worker in inland waterways or a lake transport worker on board sea-going fishing vessels.

There are special provisions that limit the hours that young workers[7] can work. The working time of a young worker must not exceed eight hours a day or 40 hours a week, and no young worker (with a few exceptions) can be employed to work between 10 p.m. and 6 a.m. (or if agreed, between 11 p.m. and 7 a.m.).

What is 'working time'?

Working time includes regular duties as well as:

- job-related training
- job-related travelling time, for example if you are a sales rep

6 Information from www.direct.gov.uk (Crown Copyright)
7 Young workers are under 18 but over school leaving age (i.e. beyond the end of the academic year of their 16th birthday)

- working lunches, such as business lunches
- time spent working abroad, if you work for a UK-based company
- paid and some unpaid overtime
- time spent on-call at the workplace.

It does not include breaks where no work is done (such as lunch), travel between home and work, time on-call away from the workplace, travelling outside work hours, unpaid overtime you have volunteered for, paid or unpaid holiday and non-job related training, e.g. evening classes or day-release courses.

Some employees are excluded from these provisions, and there are some situations that may be exempt from different parts of the provision (for example, seasonal workers in the run-up to Christmas, or workers in sectors where the work cannot be interrupted on technical grounds such as with electricity production and transmission, or the fire service).

Every worker, whether part-time or full-time, is entitled to 5.6 weeks' paid annual leave (holiday).

There are legal rights to time off work for public duties and other functions, not all of which need be paid for by the employer.

There are specific rights and responsibilities that apply in the case of maternity and parental leave.

Rest breaks

Most workers have the right to take breaks, but whether or not you are paid for them depends on the terms of your employment contract.

Types of breaks

There are different kinds of breaks from work. These include:

- **rest breaks** (e.g. lunch breaks, short breaks during the day). Adult workers can have a 20-minute break if they expect to work six hours (this may be your coffee or lunch break). It can be spent away from the workplace and should be taken in one block, somewhere in the middle of your working time. Your employer can say when the break must be taken.
- **daily rest** (the break between one work day and the next – for most people, overnight). This break should be at least 11 hours for adult workers.
- **weekly rest** (when you don't come in to work for full days, e.g. the weekend). This should be a minimum of an uninterrupted 24 hours a week or an uninterrupted 48 hours a fortnight for adult workers.

What you should know

- The amount of break time you get is usually agreed with your employer (this may be in writing, or just your employer's standard practice).
- There are minimum rest breaks required by law that your employer should give you. Your employer might have to give you longer than required if this reduces a health and safety risk.
- The short rest breaks during the day are often paid (but they don't have to be unless your contract says so). Unless you have to remain on call, daily rest and weekly rest aren't paid.

There are some exceptions to the regulations for some specific job types (such as armed forces, mobile workers and rail workers). The break rules may also apply differently to you if you travel long distances to work, do security/surveillance, constantly work in different places, or work in an industry with busy peak periods or a requirement for round-the-clock staffing. They may also be different in an emergency or risk of accident.

Over to you

You will need to know about your working hours and the steps you should take to ask for time off work, including the organisation's policies that apply to time off work for different reasons.

Task 10

What is 'working time'?

Task 11

What are the maximum hours you are allowed to work if you are aged between 16 and 17?

Hours per day:	
Hours per week:	

Task 12

How many days of paid holiday a year are you entitled to if you work:

a five-day week:	
a three-day week:	
a two-day week:	

1.6 MATERNITY/PATERNITY, PARENTAL AND ADOPTION LEAVE[8]

What you should know

If you become a parent, you will be entitled to a period of maternity, paternity and/or parental leave, which can be paid or unpaid.

- Employers cannot automatically dismiss a woman because she is pregnant.
- All pregnant employees are entitled to take up to one year's (52 weeks) maternity leave, regardless of length of service with the employer, but only 39 weeks are paid for.
- Statutory Maternity Pay (SMP) is paid for 39 weeks:
  - for the first six weeks at 90% of your average weekly earning
  - for the remaining 33 weeks, the standard rate or a rate equal to 90% of your average weekly earning (whichever is lower)
  - the standard rate from April 2009 is £124.88 per week.
- To qualify for maternity leave, you must be employed by the same employer continuously for at least 26 weeks into the 15th week before the week your baby is due.
- The notice a woman must give if she is changing her date of return from maternity leave is eight weeks.

8 Information from www.direct.gov.uk (Crown Copyright)

- Optional keeping in touch (KIT) days have been introduced enabling a woman to work for up to 10 days during her maternity leave period.
- All women have a right to return to work after maternity leave, regardless of the size of the employer.

Paternity leave

New fathers can take either one week's or two consecutive weeks' paternity leave, and during this time may be entitled to paternity pay. However, you cannot take odd days off and, if you take two weeks, they must be taken together.

The Additional Paternity Leave Regulations from April 2010 entitle male employees who are fathers, partners of mothers or adopters to take up to 26 weeks' paternity leave in the first year of the child's life or its placement for adoption.

This means that the father can share maternity leave with the mother who will be able to return to work anytime after six months, enabling the father to have what remains of the 12 months' maternity leave period.

Parental leave

Parental leave is a right to take time off work to look after a child or make arrangements for the child's welfare. It is subject to certain criteria. Parents can use it to spend more time with children and strike a better balance between work and family commitments.

Employees get 13 weeks in total for each child. Parents of disabled children get 18 weeks in total. However, strict rules apply to how much can be taken in any given year and it is only available until the child reaches five years of age or until the adopted child has been placed for five years or until the adopted child reaches 18. Parents of a disabled child can take their 18 weeks until the child reaches 18.

Parents can take leave in blocks of one week up to a maximum of four weeks in any given year. Parents of a disabled child can take the leave in periods of one day at a time.

Over to you

Task 13

How much maternity leave are mothers entitled to and how is it paid?

1.	
2.	
3.	

Task 14

What condition applies for you to qualify to receive Statutory Maternity Pay?

Task 15

How much paternity leave are fathers officially entitled to?

Task 16

What is parental leave and how long is it for?

Time off for dependants

There are allowances for you to take a reasonable amount of unpaid leave in order to handle an emergency relating to someone who depends on you. An employer can't penalise you for this if your reasons for taking this leave are genuine.

A dependant could include your husband, wife, partner, child, parent, or anyone living in your household as a member of the family, or someone who reasonably relies on you for help in an emergency.

1.7 ABSENCE AND SICKNESS[9]

What you should know

Employees have a right to receive statutory sick pay if they meet certain criteria. Some employers go beyond this and pay additional entitlements if employees are unwell.

Employees are allowed by their employers to 'self certificate' the first seven days of their sickness without the need to get a certificate from their local doctor. However, these arrangements may vary from employer to employer.

Doctors' 'sick notes' have been replaced with 'fit notes', or 'Statements of Fitness for Work'. This means that your doctor can let you know how your condition affects your ability to work. This will help your employer to understand how they might be able to help you return to work sooner. Your doctor can:

- advise when you may be fit for work with some support
- suggest common ways to help you return to work
- give information on how your condition will affect what you can do.

Over to you

You will need to know about your organisation's requirements for giving notice of absence, notification of sickness if you are unable to go to work because of ill-health, the arrangements for sick pay and the procedures you need to follow when you return to work after an illness.

9 Information from www.direct.gov.uk (Crown Copyright)

Task 17

What is the statutory level of sick pay?

1.8 DATA PROTECTION AND ACCESS TO PERSONAL INFORMATION

What you should know

The Data Protection Act gives individuals the right to know what information is held about them, including the right to find out what personal information is held on computer and most paper records. When part of your job requires you to process personal information about others, a short checklist, like the one below, will help you comply with the Data Protection Act.

Being able to answer 'yes' to every question does not guarantee compliance, and you may need more advice in particular areas, but it should mean that you are heading in the right direction.

1. Is sensitive personal data kept separate from other personal data?
2. Do the people whose information I hold know that I've got it, and are they likely to understand what it will be used for?
3. If I'm asked to pass on personal information, would the people about whom I hold information expect me to do this?
4. Am I satisfied the information is being held securely, whether it's on paper or on computer?
5. Is access to personal information limited to those with a strict need to know?
6. Am I sure the personal information is accurate and up to date?
7. Do I delete or destroy personal information as soon as I have no more need for it?
8. Have I received sufficient training from my employer in carrying out my duties and responsibilities under the Data Protection Act, and am I putting them into practice?

Over to you

Apart from knowing your rights as an individual, you will also need to know your legal obligations in the workplace and be able to comply with the requirements of the Data Protection Act.

Task 18

Provide an answer to **three** of the eight questions from the above checklist. An example is given for Question 5.

Question 5	Yes, only the HR manager is authorised to see confidential personal information

Task 19

How do you exercise your right to access your personnel records? Ask your employer and list below.

1.9 HEALTH AND SAFETY

What you should know

The Health and Safety at Work Act (1974) is the main legislation covering health and safety in the workplace.

Under this act, employers and employees have certain responsibilities, as follows.

- Employers must safeguard, as far as is reasonably practicable, the health, safety and welfare at work of all the people who work for them. This applies in particular to the provision and maintenance of a safe plant and safe systems of work and covers all machinery, equipment and substances used.
- People at work (employees) have a duty to take reasonable care to avoid harm to themselves or to others by their work activities, and to co-operate with employers and others in meeting statutory requirements. Employees must not interfere with or misuse anything provided to protect their health, safety or welfare.
- There are many health and safety regulations and codes of practice, which relate to different kinds of work and different sorts of workplaces.
- There are specific health and safety requirements relating to the employment of young people.

Over to you

You will need to know about:

- The specific health and safety regulations and codes of practice that apply to your workplace and job and the equipment you use.
- You will need to know about the measures put in place by your employer to provide protection for you and others, e.g. the name of the person who is responsible for health and safety in your workplace and your personal responsibilities.

2. PROCEDURES AND DOCUMENTS WITHIN YOUR ORGANISATION

2.1 CONTRACTS OF EMPLOYMENT

What you should know

- Your own contract of employment and/or written terms and conditions statement.
- The grievance procedures that should be followed in your own workplace.
- The system of payments used in your workplace and the associated documents.

Over to you

As already outlined in *1. Statutory rights and responsibilities* of this section, you will need to know the main terms and conditions of your contract of employment and who to go to if you have a grievance. You also need to know what information you have on your payslip, how often you are paid, and by what method.

Task 20

List three items that appear on your payslip and explain briefly what they mean (for example, National Insurance Number, National Tax Code).

1.	
2.	
3.	

2.2 ANTI-DISCRIMINATION

What you should know

- Equal opportunities policies and procedures in your workplace.
- The steps you should take if you experience or witness discrimination or bullying at work.

Task 21

Identify the legislation that exists to protect you against harassment in the workplace.

2.3 WORKING HOURS AND HOLIDAY ENTITLEMENTS

What you should know

- The working hours for your role and rest periods to which you are entitled.
- Steps you should take to request a period of time off work and the organisation's rules that apply to time off work for different reasons.

Over to you

You will need to know what hours you are supposed to work, your shifts (if applicable), what time you are allowed for breaks and how you go about asking for time off for various reasons.

Task 22

Who do you need to contact to request time off work?

2.4 SICKNESS ABSENCE AND SICK PAY

What you should know

- Organisational sick pay arrangements relevant to your occupation.
- The rules about how and when you must notify your employer if you are unable to come to work because of ill-health, and the implications of not following these.

Over to you

You will need to know about the organisation's rules for giving notice of absence, notification if you are unable to go to work because of sickness and the arrangements for sick pay. You also need to know what will happen if you do not follow these rules.

Task 23

What are the arrangements for notification of sickness in your organisation? (For example, do you need to contact your place of work before a specific time on your first day of absence?)

2.5 DATA PROTECTION

What you should know

- Who you report to on matters to do with your personnel record.
- The procedure to follow to report any changes in your circumstances.
- The type of information that is in your personnel record and who has access to it.

Over to you

You will need to know who to inform if you have a change of circumstances, such as address change or change of name. You also need to know what information is kept about you and who has a right to see that information.

WorkSkills Unit 2: 2.4

Task 24

List three examples of changes to your personal circumstances that would need to be reported to your employer. Who would you report these changes to?

1.	Report to whom:
2.	Report to whom:
3.	Report to whom:

2.6 HEALTH AND SAFETY

What you should know

- The specific health and safety regulations and codes of practice that apply to your workplace and job.
- The measures put in place by your employer to provide protection for you and others against any risks arising from the work carried out, the environment, or the tools, materials or equipment used.

Over to you

You will need to know of any regulations and codes of practice on health and safety that apply to your job, how you help to keep yourself and others safe in the workplace, and how your work complies with those requirements.

Task 25

Give one example of a health and safety regulation and explain why it applies to your workplace.

Task 26

Who is the nominated person in your workplace responsible for the first aid arrangements?

Name:	
Job title:	

3. SOURCES OF INFORMATION AND ADVICE ABOUT EMPLOYMENT RIGHTS AND RESPONSIBILITIES

3.1 INTERNAL SOURCES

What you should know

- The range of information made available to you by your employer on matters relating to your employment and working practice.
- Where this information can be obtained.

Over to you

You will need to know who to go to for information and advice in your organisation. This can be on a range of topics related to:

- employment and personnel issues
- training
- additional learning support
- assessment.

WorkSkills Unit 2: 1.4

Task 27

Where would you find information within your organisation about:

1.	Personnel issues (e.g. annual leave entitlement)
2.	Training opportunities (e.g. in-house training, qualifications)
3.	Additional learning support (e.g. for a learning difficulty, medical condition or disability)

3.2 EXTERNAL SOURCES

What you should know

- Other information sources that may be available outside the workplace, what they provide and how to use them.

Over to you

You will need to know where to go for information outside your organisation. This can be obtained from a range of sources, such as:

- the Citizens Advice Bureau
- trade unions
- Access to Work contact centres.

Task 28

Which external source(s) would you turn to for information relating to:

1.	*Health and safety at work*
2.	*Equal opportunities*
3.	*Data protection*
4.	*Access to Work*

4. ABOUT YOUR OCCUPATION AND ORGANISATION

What you should know

- The type of organisation you work for, in terms of the following factors:
  - the number of people they employ
  - the type of market in which they operate
  - whether there are any issues of public concern that affect your organisation and/or industry.
- The types of changes that have been taking place in your area of business over recent years, which have affected individual's working practices and the way in which organisations operate.
- The impact, if any, that these changes have had on your organisation and the way in which your job role is carried out.
- How your organisation is structured.
- The different ways in which organisations carry out different tasks, such as finance, operations, personnel, marketing, health and safety etc.
- The different ways in which the tasks outlined above may be split between different people, departments and/or sites.
- What steps you should take to try to ensure you interact effectively with colleagues and contacts in the workplace and why this is important to the organisation.

Over to you

Job roles vary from one organisation to the next and have faced many changes over recent years that have affected working practices and the way in which organisations operate.

Task 29

What are the main changes that have taken place in your area of business over the last few years? You may wish to think about some of the changes in technology or the centralisation of tasks, for instance. List at least three changes.

1.	

Continued overleaf

2.	
3.	

WorkSkills Unit 2: 3.2

Task 30

Give an example of how any of the changes in Task 29 have affected roles within your organisation.

Task 31

Describe the main tasks that are part of your job role. List a maximum of four.

1.	
2.	

CfA ERR WORKBOOK

3.	
4.	

Task 32

Draw a chart of your organisation (or department), everyone's job roles and who they report to. Make sure you include yourself. If your organisation already has a chart, amend it to include yourself.

5. OCCUPATIONS AND CAREER PATHWAYS

What you should know

- That occupations may be specialised to a particular industry, for example car manufacturing, website design or banking.
- The requirements and characteristics of typical career paths associated with your occupation.
- The main stages and requirements of the development programme you are pursuing and what training and development opportunities your organisation provides in relation to this.

Over to you

You need to know what opportunities are available to you and the different career paths you can take and how to access them. You need to know about training and development and how this can progress your career.

Task 33

WorkSkills Unit 11: 3.2

List the opportunities for training and development provided by your employer (for example short courses, in-house training, etc).

Task 34

Who in your workplace can you discuss these options with?

Name:	
Job title:	

6. REPRESENTATIVE BODIES RELEVANT TO YOU AND YOUR ORGANISATION

6.1 REPRESENTATION

Within any industry, there is a range of representative bodies that promote the views of a group of people with common interests.

The representative bodies collect the views of their members and act as their collective voice in discussions with other groups on issues that affect them all. Representation occurs both within an organisation and in other bodies. Representation between different bodies can occur at local and national levels as well.

What you should know

You should know:

- if there are any trade unions relevant to your occupation, in representing and protecting the common interests of employees
- if there are any professional bodies relevant to your occupation
- if there are any regulatory bodies relevant to your industry and occupation, for example the British Medical Association
- of the name and role of the standards setting organisation relevant to your occupation.

Over to you

You will need to know the names and roles of your standards setting organisation, any professional/representative or regulatory bodies, trade unions, consumer groups and employer organisations.

Task 35

Describe the role and purpose of the Health and Safety Executive.

Task 36

State what the main trade union is for your occupation and what it does.

Task 37

Name the standards setting organisation in your area of business and explain briefly what it does.

7. ERR EVIDENCE RECORD CHECKLIST

Task number	Completed	Comments
1	☐	
2	☐	
3	☐	
4	☐	
5	☐	
6	☐	
7	☐	
8	☐	
9	☐	
10	☐	
11	☐	
12	☐	
13	☐	
14	☐	
15	☐	
16	☐	
17	☐	
18	☐	

cfa business skills @ work

Task number	Completed	Comments
19	☐	
20	☐	
21	☐	
22	☐	
23	☐	
24	☐	
25	☐	
26	☐	
27	☐	
28	☐	
29	☐	
30	☐	
31	☐	
32	☐	
33	☐	
34	☐	
35	☐	
36	☐	
37	☐	

cfa business skills @ work

COMPLETION OF THE BTEC APPRENTICESHIP ASSESSMENT WORKBOOK ERR SECTION

Framework	
Business & Administration	
Contact Centre	
Customer Service	
Marketing & Communication	
Sales & Telesales	
Team Leading & Management	

We, the undersigned, agree that the knowledge and understanding covered in the employment rights and responsibilities section of this Workbook, developed by the CfA, has been completed by the apprentice named below.

Apprentice details	
Name of apprentice	
Date of birth	
Signature	
Candidate number	
Name of employer/line manager	
Signature	

Training provider details	
Name of training provider	
Address	
Postcode	

A copy of this page should be retained in the Workbook. The original (signed) version should be returned to the CfA upon completion of the relevant framework, with copies of all the evidence required.

cfa business skills @ work